RAND NATIONAL SECURITY

New SECURITY and JUSTICE SECTOR Partnership Models

IMPLICATIONS OF THE ARAB UPRISINGS

Michael J. McNerney, Jennifer D. P. Moroney,
Peter Mandaville, Terry Hagen

Prepared for the State Department Bureau of Political-Military Affairs

This research was conducted within the International Security and Defense Policy Center of the RAND National Security Research Division (NSRD). NSRD conducts research and analysis on defense and national security topics for U.S. and allied defense, foreign policy, homeland security, and intelligence communities and foundations, as well as other nongovernmental organizations that support defense and national security analysis.

Library of Congress Cataloging-in-Publication Data is available for this publication.

ISBN: 978-0-8330-8575-7

Cover photo by AP Photo/Christophe Ena

Text with original: "Flowers are put in the barrel of a soldier's weapon by protestors in front of the RCD party headquarters, in Tunis, Thursday, Jan. 20. 2011. Demonstrators have criticized the country's new unity government for being mostly made up of old guard politicians from the RCD party, which was founded by ousted President Zine El Abidine Ben Ali, who fled to Saudi Arabia on Friday after 23 years in power."

RAND OFFICES

SANTA MONICA, CA • WASHINGTON, DC

PITTSBURGH, PA • NEW ORLEANS, LA • JACKSON, MS • BOSTON, MA

CAMBRIDGE, UK • BRUSSELS, BE

www.rand.org

Preface

The United States faces an important set of challenges and opportunities in strengthening security and justice sector partnerships in the Middle East and North Africa. The emergence of a series of popular uprisings in the Arab world since 2010 complicates these efforts, while making their success all the more important.

The State Department asked RAND's National Security Research Division to analyze potential new partnership models that could help implement recent policy guidance related to improving security and justice sector assistance and promoting reform in this region.

This research was conducted within the International Security and Defense Policy Center of the RAND National Security Research Division (NSRD). NSRD conducts research and analysis on defense and national security topics for U.S. and allied defense, foreign policy, homeland security, and intelligence communities and foundations, as well as other nongovernmental organizations that support defense and national security analysis.

For more information on the International Security and Defense Policy Center, see http://www.rand.org/nsrd/ndri/centers/isdp.html or contact the Director (contact information is provided on the web page).

Contents

Figures and Tables

Figures

Tables

Summary

Two U.S. policy shifts are raising important questions for those involved in managing relationships with foreign partners in the security and justice sector. The first shift began with the development of the State Department's *Quadrennial Diplomacy and Development Review* (QDDR) and intensified with the Presidential Policy Directive (PPD) on Security Sector Assistance (SSA). These documents emphasized improving foreign assistance through planning, assessments, interagency integration, and partner-nation ownership. The second shift began in response to the Arab Uprisings of 2010–2011, with new policy guidance emphasizing the need for U.S. agencies to promote political and security sector reform with partner nations in the Middle East and North Africa (MENA). Sound planning and promotion of reform are, of course, not new policies, but their emphasis has clearly grown, challenging status quo approaches to U.S. partnerships with foreign partners. But how do these shifts translate into real changes in security and justice sector (SJS) assistance, particularly when dealing with the complexities of the MENA region?

The State Department asked RAND to perform three tasks: (1) assess current approaches to U.S. SJS assistance in the MENA region; (2) develop new models for SJS partnerships, integrating U.S. security and reform objectives; and (3) identify concrete and actionable options.

The data on U.S. assistance and MENA country characteristics defied simplistic descriptions. SJS assistance relies on a complex web of programs and organizations that must be tailored to address the nuanced characteristics and interests of partner countries. Contrary to conventional wisdom, our research did not find that security assistance programs like foreign military financing (FMF) provided the United States with extensive leverage over its partners. Most MENA partners make more purchases of U.S. equipment and services through foreign military sales than they receive in FMF. Moreover, those countries that receive high amounts of assistance are generally crucial partners in counterterrorism, regional stability, and other efforts important to U.S. interests. Conversely, we also did not find that security assistance programs provide MENA partners with excessive leverage over the United States. They truly value these relationships and do not see engagement as a purely transactional activity. U.S. SJS assistance—and engagement efforts more generally—are central to maintaining strong relationships based on mutual respect. This report argues that promoting reform and achieving other U.S. objectives are more likely to succeed through an emphasis on identifying and pursuing common interests rather than through rewards and threats.

Understanding how to pursue common interests as they relate to political and SJS reform, however, is particularly challenging in the MENA region. As our data showed, MENA countries score poorly on state governance relative to every other region in the world, based on several indexes. But we also found that MENA partners show important variations relative to each other. There are many aspects to understanding a state's levels of fragility, its respect for rule of law, levels of personal autonomy, etc., so it would be a mistake to assume that every country in the region is equally dysfunctional in every category of governance. U.S. partnership efforts are more likely to be effective when based on models that account for these variations and build on those areas of greatest promise.

We evaluated new partnership models by analyzing opportunities, challenges, and best practices. Although we began with three hypothetical partnership models, we ultimately settled on a hybrid model that drew on the most useful elements of all three. The data we analyzed and the interviews we conducted led us to the conclusion that "three sizes fit all" could be no more effective than "one size fits all." Instead, we designed our single model—the Enhanced Partnership Planning (EPP) Model, which focuses on improving collaborative planning, rather than on influencing partner nations to do what the United States wants—to serve as a flexible framework that could support tailored, rigorous SJS planning by U.S. and partner nation stakeholders.

The EPP Model emphasizes several opportunities that were highlighted during our research.

- First, we found many SJS stakeholders working toward more integrated planning, in accordance with QDDR and SSA PPD guidance. For example, officials were breaking down stovepipes between security sector and justice sector planning within the U.S. government. Moreover, officials were shifting from assistance-based or sales-based mindsets to true partnership mindsets that included partner ownership of planning. Finally, we also saw opportunities—often underexploited—for coordination among other donors and actors in the region, such as the United Kingdom.
- Second, we found evidence that many MENA partners are indeed interested in building more effective and professional security and justice sectors. While this does not equate to allowing imposition of U.S. standards on partner forces, it indicated that opportunities exist to help partners professionalize their own forces in important ways.
- Third, we found the potential for implementing an EPP Model, through pilot efforts with selected partners who are receptive to a more sophisticated approach to measuring and communicating progress toward concrete objectives. U.S. officials could jointly develop performance metrics with these partner nations on a limited set of SJS objectives, then monitor and evaluate progress against partner-owned benchmarks.

The potential opportunities we identified in support of the EPP Model were tempered by several challenges.

- First, ongoing U.S. security interests frequently threaten to constrain reform initiatives. Our interviews indicated that the most

promising way to overcome this challenge lay not in one set of objectives trumping another but in finding win-win approaches.
- Second, despite many efforts to improve SJS partnerships, there often exists a temptation to continue "business as usual" approaches. Many stakeholders were particularly concerned about partner perceptions that disruptive changes might be imposed unilaterally by the United States.
- Third, given the variation in SJS relationships and the challenges in predicting partner nation reactions to change, U.S. efforts to exert leverage on partners could be politically dangerous.
- Fourth, incentives to integrate U.S. activities with those of allies and donors in the region were not always clear. Despite the potential benefits of U.S. collaboration with other actors, information-sharing appeared to substitute at times for coordinated planning.
- Fifth, congressional interests add to the complexity of any efforts to implement changes to SJS and other partnership activities in the MENA region.

Finally, the EPP Model benefits from several best practices we identified in our research.

- First, two of the QDDR's components of partnerships may apply well to SJS, focusing on (1) country ownership, with partner countries taking the lead in developing and implementing strategies; and (2) mutual accountability, creating mechanisms for meaningful commitments by both partner countries and donors.
  - The Department of State's Bureau of International Narcotics and Law Enforcement Affairs, the U.S. Agency for International Development, and the Millennium Challenge Corporation have all identified best practices in the areas of partner country ownership and mutual accountability through development of benchmarks.
- Second, prior studies and several interviewees emphasized the importance of human capacity development, both to strengthen good governance and to build trust and foster resilience in the face of crises.

- Third, deliberate strategic planning exercises can help translate monitoring and evaluation efforts into programming changes.

Our analysis led to recommendations in the areas of planning, assessments, and resources. Based on our analysis of U.S. assistance in the MENA region, the characteristics of MENA countries, and potential new partnership models, we shared several pages of findings in Chapter Four. Along with these findings, we provide several recommendations in the following three areas:

Planning:

- Establish a formalized structure for SJS discussions in specific sectors. Regular planning meetings under this structure would help integrate SJS stakeholders across the board.
- Establish integrated country strategies (ICSs) as the focus of regular discussions about joint objectives and SJS partnership (SJSP) activities.
- Identify likely resource constraints as early as possible and mitigate negative effects. Mitigation can be accomplished, for example, by working with other stakeholders to leverage each other's efforts.

Assessing:

- Come to mutual agreement, through dialogue with partner nations and based on common analysis of security sector priorities and needs, regarding key sectors and program areas that merit assessment to maximize outcomes and mutual benefit.
- Once key SJSP sectors have been identified, apply SMART criteria (specific, measurable, attainable, results-oriented, time-bound) to identify the possible metrics for assessing programs.
- Together with the partner nation, select a pilot project on a topic of mutual interest in the security and justice sectors.
- Work with partner nation to identify specific benchmarks and timeline milestones ("check-in points") for the target project that

both the United States and partner nation can use to assess performance and progress.
- Where appropriate and where the broader bilateral relationship permits, consider formalizing the benchmarks and milestones in a written document.
- Integrate these steps and actions into ICSs to ensure that they reflect and remain deconflicted with broader U.S. strategic goals in the partner nation.

Resourcing:
- Ensure assessment results reach resource managers and associated recommendations in time to inform their decisions.
- Ensure resource managers take part in planning and assessing meetings with the partner.
- Communicate using a Memorandum of Understanding (MOU) or other more formal communique.

As is clear from the ongoing events in Egypt, Syria, and a number of other countries implicated in the Arab uprisings, the United States is likely to face a highly fluid political and security environment for a number of years. The central impulse behind the uprisings—popular demands for accountable and effective governance—raises questions about whether the United States should explore ways to reflect greater emphasis on reform in its MENA security and justice sector partnerships. Against this regional backdrop, the U.S. government is rolling out new policy guidance relating to foreign assistance more broadly and SSA more specifically. Our research provides a framework that can support security and justice sector assistance strategists and planners as they seek to implement new policy guidelines that integrate elements of accountability and reform while continuing to track core U.S. interests and equities in a rapidly evolving regional context.

Acknowledgments

We deeply appreciate the assistance provided by our sponsor, Art Collins, and his Department of State colleagues who gave generously of their time and facilitated our access to information. In particular, we thank the U.S. country teams in Egypt and Bahrain for hosting our visits and the teams in Saudi Arabia, the United Arab Emirates, Yemen, and Morocco for speaking with us. Many State Department officials in Political-Military Affairs, Near Eastern Affairs, International Narcotics and Law Enforcement, and the Office of Policy Planning also gave generously of their time. We are also grateful for the insights provided by officials from the U.S. Agency for International Development, the Office of the Secretary of Defense, U.S. Navy Fifth Fleet, Millennium Challenge Corporation, Government of Bahrain, and the United Kingdom Ministry of Defence, Foreign and Commonwealth Office, and Embassy in Bahrain. Finally, we appreciate insights from Dr. Philip R. Fletcher and officials at the International Institute for Strategic Studies and several other nongovernmental organizations.

We also recognize the invaluable contributions of several of our RAND colleagues. Emma Davies Cutrufello was instrumental collecting and analyzing the data for Chapter Two. Beth Grill, Jeff Martini, and Ali Nader also provided important insights on U.S. assistance programs and the Middle East region. We also acknowledge the insightful leadership and guidance of James Dobbins and Eric Peltz, directors of RAND's International Security and Defense Policy Center.

We also thank our reviewers, Tamara Wittes and Charles Ries, whose comments were extremely helpful in making our report more accurate, clearer, and more insightful.

Finally, we recognize the indispensable administrative support provided by Jocqueline Johnson and Jennie Breon.

Abbreviations

EPP	Enhanced Partnership Planning
FMF	foreign military financing
FMS	foreign military sales
FSI	Failed States Index
GDP	gross domestic product
ICS	Integrated Country Strategy
IMET	International Military Education and Training
ISAB	International Security Advisory Board
MCC	Millennium Challenge Corporation
MENA	Middle East and North Africa
MOA	memorandum of agreement
MOU	memorandum of understanding
MSRP	Mission Strategic and Resource Plan
PfG	Partnership for Growth
PPD	presidential policy directive
QDDR	Quadrennial Diplomacy and Development Review
SFI	State Fragility Index

SJS	security and justice sector
SJSA	security and justice sector assistance
SJSP	security and justice sector partnership
SMART	specific, measurable, attainable, results-oriented, time-bound
SSA	security sector assistance
USAID	U.S. Agency for International Development

CHAPTER ONE

Introduction

Those charged with designing and implementing U.S. security cooperation programs in the Middle East and North Africa (MENA) region find themselves at a crossroads. Over the course of the past three years, major shifts in the political landscape of the Arab world have coincided with the announcement of significant shifts in U.S. foreign and national security policy—quite independent of regional events, and in some cases, predating them.

The Arab uprisings that began in Tunisia in 2010 and spread to Egypt, Bahrain, Yemen, Libya, and Syria the following year have already claimed several longstanding regimes and ushered in a combination of new and unfamiliar governments, civil war and humanitarian crises, and enormous political volatility amid ongoing socioeconomic malaise. Just prior to these regional shocks, the U.S. State Department issued a blueprint for how to approach statecraft in the 21st century in the form of the first *Quadrennial Diplomacy and Development Review* (QDDR). For the past several years, White House national security staff have been carrying out an ongoing review of U.S. security sector assistance (SSA), which resulted in a presidential policy directive (PPD) in April 2013.

The confluence of these various developments offers a combination of challenges and opportunities in the realm of U.S. security cooperation. Those within the State Department who oversee SSA programs in MENA are faced with a dual challenge: Not only are they being asked by the QDDR and PPD to conceptualize security assistance in new ways, they are asked to do so in a highly volatile region where aspects of longstanding U.S. strategic calculus may be shifting. On the one hand, a new regional environment forces the United States to reexamine its security commitments in the Middle East and to ask whether current partnerships are in keeping with its own strategic interests going forward—as well as those of its partner nations. More specifically, to what extent are current SSA approaches advancing longer-term U.S. goals in the region, and to what extent do they hamper progress on these objectives? On the other hand, the fact that a new regional reality is emerging (along with a broader discussion of U.S. SSA policy) provides an impetus and opportunity to revisit—perhaps with a view to revising—long-engrained ways of doing business in the Arab world.

Study Objectives

The purpose of this report is to provide a framework for thinking through the implications of the Arab uprisings for how the United States approaches SSA in the MENA region—even as SSA policy parameters seem to be in motion. Based on research and interviews spanning Washington, D.C., regional posts, partner nations, and other allies, we advance a set of specific recommendations that can help guide strategic planning for U.S. security assistance in the Middle East as well as other global settings.

Prioritizing Stability over Democracy in MENA

The Arab uprisings that began in 2010 have thrown into stark relief a longstanding dictum governing U.S. conduct in the Arab world—namely, the idea that there is both an inherent tension and a zero-sum relationship between U.S. strategic interests and U.S. support for reform in the region. Moreover, the general assumption has been that the former always takes precedence over the latter. While democracy promotion has held a consistent spot on the docket of U.S. interests in the Middle East for many years, it has tended to fall farther down the list relative to other perceived imperatives, such as containing Iran, counterterrorism, energy security, and defending regional allies. Viewed from Washington, D.C., this policy course—which has enjoyed a remarkable bipartisan consensus over several decades—appears to be a prudent and measured means to ensure U.S. strategic interests and regional stability. Viewed from the Middle East, however, this approach has created a conviction in the minds of many in the Arab world that Washington's pursuit of its national security has served as a handmaiden to authoritarianism and bad governance. The initial U.S. hesitation over Egypt as mass demonstrations gathered force there in January 2011 and the perceived lack of serious pressure on Bahrain's government after the killing of numerous protestors were both viewed through this lens by observers in the region.[1]

Close relationships between Washington and the governments of key allies have been central to preserving U.S. strategic equities in the Middle East over the years. In several cases—such as Egypt, Jordan, and the Arab Gulf states—the development of something akin to special strategic relationships has been facilitated in important ways by various forms of security cooperation with the United States. While cash transfers and procurement-related activity has certainly been a mainstay of these efforts, they also extend more broadly to operational activities such as joint exercises, training and professional development programs, and exchange initiatives designed to build trust and greater human interoperability between the U.S. military and the armed services of key partner nations in the region. Put together, these activities are seen to serve both the direct force posture and operational needs of U.S. security interests—such as overflight rights, facility access, and counterterrorism cooperation—as well as to function in important ways at the symbolic level. Generally absent from this domain, however, has been any effort to link security cooperation—and the various forms of direct U.S. financial assistance it often entails—to security sector reforms in partner countries.

Dramatic shifts in the Middle East resulting from the Arab uprisings and associated efforts on the part of the United States to reorient

---

[1] See Shibley Telhami, *The World Through Arab Eyes: Arab Public Opinion and the Reshaping of the Middle East*, New York: Basic Books, 2013.

itself in the region suggest that it may be time to take a closer look at the relationship between security cooperation and the kinds of reforms the United States now believes are conducive to longer-term stability. It may be necessary to think differently about U.S. interests in the MENA region, focusing on the question of what would best achieve long-term stability and security rather than emphasizing narrowly defined short-term security needs. While challenges associated with Iran and freedom of navigation through key strategic channels (e.g., Suez, Hormuz) rightfully guide U.S. calculations in the region, recent events also demonstrate the need to strike a balance between efforts to animate modest reform and the temptation to reject change as something inherently antithetical to the advancement of U.S. security.

Reform as a Strategic Necessity and the Role of SSA

In the aftermath of the popular revolutions that toppled dictators in Tunisia, Egypt, and Libya—not to mention a leadership change in Yemen, some measure of constitutional reform in Morocco, and violent protests in Bahrain and Syria—the United States has sought to emphasize the need to find a "new way of doing business" in the Middle East. Successive policy statements and speeches by U.S. government principals since 2011 have emphasized renewed U.S. support for democracy in the region. On May 19, 2011, President Barack Obama declared that "it will be the policy of the United States to promote reform across the region and to support transitions to democracy."[2] In November 2011, then–Secretary of State Hillary Rodham Clinton directly engaged and rejected the idea that there is a necessary trade-off between security and democracy in the Middle East by saying that, "the greatest single source of instability in today's Middle East is not the demand for change. It is the refusal to change."[3]

[2] The White House, "Remarks by the President on the Middle East and North Africa," May 19, 2011.

[3] U.S. Department of State, "Keynote Address at the National Democratic Institute's 2011 Democracy Awards Dinner," Remarks by Hillary Rodham Clinton, November 7, 2011.

Such statements reflect the fact that, at some level, the U.S. strategic calculus in the region is evolving in light of recent events. It is important to note that the U.S. administration did not discover its concerns about Middle East authoritarianism overnight in the wake of the 2011 uprisings. Speaking on behalf of the Bush administration in 2005, then–Secretary of State Condoleezza Rice sounded many of the same concerns about resistance to reform. But such statements were rarely reflected in concrete policy actions. For several decades, successive U.S. administrations preferred to support leaders willing to cooperate in advancing American security interests in the region, with relatively little regard for their conduct in the domestic realm. Years of popular discontent over ineffective and unaccountable governance eventually reached such a clear boiling point that even before the Arab uprisings erupted, Clinton warned regional regimes that they needed to change or risk "sinking into the sand."[4] The revolutions that swept the region in 2011 led the U.S. administration to revisit some of its assumptions about stability and security in the Arab world. If American security interests were dependent on the perseverance of increasingly precarious autocratic regimes, then the seeds of instability were sown into the very system on which the United States had been relying for years. Viewed in this light, the need for regional governments to initiate meaningful reforms becomes a cornerstone of securing long-term stability. "[O]pening political systems, societies, and economies is not simply a matter of idealism," Clinton declared. "It is a strategic necessity." The idea here is that the Arab uprisings have demonstrated that authoritarian regimes are ultimately unstable because they refuse to be responsive and accountable to populations increasingly unwilling to remain silent. By not initiating processes of political reform now, regional governments increase the likelihood that they will face internal opposition—potentially violent in nature—in the future. It is therefore in the interest of the United States to encourage these countries down the path of democracy before they become increasingly unstable.

---

[4] U.S. Department of State, "Manama Dialogue Opening Dinner," remarks by Hillary Rodham Clinton, December 3, 2010.

The U.S. administration, however, has faced considerable challenges in operationalizing this new approach. Ongoing instability and violence in the region, continued skepticism about U.S. support for democracy and civil society, and a generalized sense that American influence in the Middle East is waning have dampened U.S. government efforts to significantly alter the strategic orientation in the Arab world. But there are also drag effects generated by very real U.S. concerns, such as Gulf security imperatives (Iran) and political violence in Sinai and parts of North Africa. To date, much of the debate about how the United States can influence outcomes in the region has centered on foreign assistance—particularly the sizable amounts of military aid that go to countries such as Egypt and Israel (more than $1 billion per year) and, to a lesser extent, Iraq and Jordan. While the U.S. Congress has sought to enforce some measure of democratic conditionality over these funds, ongoing regional uncertainties as well as concerns about the structure of U.S. defense contracts with Egypt have twice led the U.S. administration to exercise national security waivers and allow military aid to Egypt to continue flowing despite clear authoritarian actions on the part of the Muslim Brotherhood-led government.[5] In July 2013, the same government was overthrown in what was widely perceived as a military coup. The subsequent violent crackdown on the Muslim Brotherhood at the hands of Egypt's security forces led the United States to first cancel the Bright Star joint military exercises and eventually to suspend several components of U.S. military aid. The controversy and debate surrounding these decisions illustrate the challenges that Washington faces today in calibrating its MENA security cooperation policies. Speaking at the United Nations General Assembly in September 2013, President Obama seemed to summarize the dilemma faced by the United States when he said that the "United States will at times work with governments that do not meet . . . the highest international expectations, but who work with us on our core interests."

---

[5] Ernesto Londoño and Holly Yeager, "In Debate over Military Aid to Egypt, Contractual Issues Loom Large for U.S.," washingtonpost.com, July 25, 2013.

Part of the problem, we find, is that efforts to use U.S. security assistance as a lever in the aftermath of the Arab uprisings have suffered from a tendency either to continue doing "business as usual" or, at the other extreme, to think in terms of coupling existing SSA approaches to a political conditionality "on-off" switch. Rather than relying on the rather blunt language of withholding or cutting off aid, a more effective and sustainable approach, our research suggests, could emerge from an effort to rethink some of the mechanisms and priorities that SSA currently comprises—particularly if and when such programs are designed with sufficient flexibility to accommodate individual country nuances and needs. Our research on current regional SSA approaches (presented in Chapter Two) reinforces one of the key findings of that study and strongly informs the recommendations we make in Chapter Three—specifically, the idea that security assistance programs focused on building human capacity—rather than raw kinetic capabilities—are some of the most effective tools for effecting sustainable reforms in the security sector and civil-military relations more broadly. Another recent study on defense cooperation with the region echoes this theme, urging the United States to "apportion less money to equipment purchases and more money to exercises, exchanges, and training—particularly IMET [international military education and training]—that will help inculcate values of transparency, accountability, and civilian control of the military."[6] This study also reflects some of the challenges identified by the broader literature on the spotty record of external actors trying to generate momentum toward reform in the justice sector, and the importance of building on the efforts of new-generation reformers in partner nations.[7]

---

6 George Casey and Jim Kolbe, *A New Deal: Reforming U.S. Defense Cooperation with Egypt, Libya, and Tunisia*, Washington, D.C.: Atlantic Council of the United States, 2013, p. 19.

7 See Rachel Kleinfeld, *Advancing the Rule of Law Abroad: Next Generation Reform*, Washington, D.C.: Carnegie Endowment for International Peace, 2012.

Accountability and Impact in U.S. Foreign Assistance

A new regional reality is not the sole impetus for rethinking U.S. SSA. Two recently released policy frameworks—the State Department's 2010 QDDR and the April 2013 PPD on SSA—mandate broad shifts in the norms, priorities, and practices that define U.S. foreign and national security policymaking. The push to implement aspects of these directives even as the region continues to be highly volatile forces MENA SSA specialists to contend with a dizzying array of pressures and demands, some of which may even appear contradictory. For the purposes of this report, we prefer to emphasize a "glass half-full" perspective. We find that many of the ideas, resources, and broad directions set by these frameworks are broadly consistent with a trajectory that can permit U.S. SSA to become more effective even as it lays the groundwork for varying degrees of lasting reform in the MENA region and beyond.

The U.S. State Department's 2010 QDDR identifies various new directions and values that should characterize U.S. development aid policy going forward. Among them is an emphasis on heightened transparency, monitoring, and evaluation of all U.S. assistance. One hallmark feature of the QDDR's approach to development aid is a shift away from the language of donor and recipient. Instead, the emphasis here lies on the idea of entering into development *partnerships*, a concept that implies mutual responsibilities and obligations. More specifically, the QDDR articulates the need to develop new models of development partnership characterized in the following terms:

- **country ownership**, with partner countries taking the lead in developing and implementing evidence-based strategies, as appropriate. In those countries where governments are strongly committed to development and democracy, country ownership means working much more closely with and through those governments; in all countries it means working closely and consulting with organizations and the people most directly affected by programs and activities.

- **mutual accountability**, creating mechanisms for meaningful commitments for action and resource allocation by both partner governments and donors.[8]

Elements of this approach have found tangible expression in the work of recent initiatives such as the Partnership for Growth (PfG) and the Millennium Challenge Corporation (MCC)—a foreign assistance agency established by the George W. Bush administration. But it has been difficult to integrate accountability and country ownership criteria into U.S. foreign assistance more broadly—a domain that traditionally has been heavily guided by political earmarks and strategic considerations. One MENA country serves as a useful illustration of the tensions inherent in trying to make aid decisions based on governance quality and accountability criteria: In 2006, the MCC controversially declared Jordan eligible for a large-scale development grant (or "compact" in MCC's terminology) even though that country did not pass the MCC's democracy criteria—a deal eventually worth some $275 million to the Hashemite Kingdom. Critics cited this as yet another example of security interests trumping support for democracy, with the United States perceived as "rewarding" Jordan for its counterterrorism cooperation.[9]

Another hallmark of the QDDR is its emphasis on "whole of government" solutions that can deploy the combined resources of multiple U.S. government agencies with relevant assets and experience. This approach involves integrating and building closer ties between domains that are traditionally seen to fall within the single remit of diplomacy, development, or defense. Addressing security and justice sector assistance specifically, the QDDR aims to:

- **integrate security- and justice-sector assistance** through comprehensive efforts, including convening core security actors, man-

---

8 U.S. Department of State and U.S. Agency for International Development (USAID), *Leading Through Civilian Power, The First Quadrennial Diplomacy and Development Review*, 2010.

9 Jeremy Sharp, "Jordan: Background and U.S. Relations," Congressional Research Service, April 9, 2010, p. 22.

agement and oversight bodies, justice institutions, and civil society.

- **adopt a whole-of-government approach** that integrates the skills of other federal agencies—and, where appropriate, state and local governments—in the design and implementation of security- and justice-sector assistance efforts.
- **link security- and justice-sector assistance to development** by emphasizing host nations' ownership of programs and supporting programs that address their concerns.[10]

Taken as a whole, these points articulate key dimensions of what has been described as a new "3D" approach to integrating the work of diplomacy, development, and defense in U.S. foreign policy.[11] This strategy also opens up the possibility of thinking about conditionality linkages between security assistance and reform efforts beyond the security and justice sectors—i.e., the idea that security cooperation could be tied to broader democratic and political reforms.

New Directions for Security and Justice Sector Assistance

The QDDR's emphasis on the need for shifting to a partnership paradigm and greater cross-governmental integration in foreign assistance efforts is reinforced by both the findings of a recent assessment of U.S. SSA as well as new policy guidance contained in the April 2013 PPD on SSA.

The State Department's International Security Advisory Board (ISAB) 2013 *Report on Security Capacity Building* represents a major strategic level assessment of U.S. SSA efforts. The report identifies a number of key challenges and imperatives facing SSA today, several of which bear directly on the objectives of this report. Among the challenges:

---

[10] U.S. Department of State and USAID, 2010, p. xv.

[11] USAID, *3D Planning Guide, Diplomacy, Development, Defense*, July 31, 2012b.

1. The United States spends some $25 billion annually in SSA designed to enhance the "security capacity" of partner nations, but without any clear operational definition of security capacity, no consistent logic for allocating funds and determining appropriate expenditure levels, and little in the way of criteria for assessing program effectiveness.[12]
2. Current SSA efforts are highly disaggregated and spread across disparate programmatic and funding mechanisms in multiple government agencies.[13]

Consistent with the linkage we identify between reform and long-term U.S. strategic interests, the report also makes the following point:

> A goal that may be of increasing significance is encouragement and fostering of reform in recipient nations' internal security institutions and their operation. The premise is that assisting nations in building security capacity that is consistent with democratic norms, human rights standards, and rule of law provides the necessary space in which development—economic, social, and political—can take place, and that such development is important to U.S. long-term interests in peace and stability.[14]

One of the main components of such an approach, the report goes on to suggest, should entail placing greater emphasis on civilian aspects of security capacity. "Providing military assistance for counterterrorism purposes without similar assistance to civilian bodies that oversee the military and to the civilian justice system may not produce the type of government structure and capabilities that the U.S. would like to see in the long term," the report argues.[15]

In April 2013 the White House issued a PPD dealing with SSA. Many of its provisions are consistent with and respond to the chal.

---

[12] ISAB, *Report on Security Capacity Building*, Washington, D.C.: U.S. Department of State, 2013, p. 1.

[13] ISAB, 2013, p. 18.

[14] ISAB, 2013, p. 18.

[15] ISAB, 2013, p. 24.

lenges and recommendations that follow from the ISAB report. For example, in the course of clarifying that the primary goal of SSA is to enhance the security capacity of partner nations and allies, the PPD emphasizes that this must be accomplished in ways that are in keeping with principles of good governance. One of the principal goals of U.S. SSA, the PPD explains, should be to "promote universal values, such as good governance, transparent and accountable oversight of security forces, rule of law, transparency, accountability, delivery of fair and effective justice, and respect for human rights."[16]

The PPD also focuses on the need for the kind of cross-sectoral linkages—or at the very least greater cross-sectoral awareness—emphasized by the QDDR and ISAB reports. It mandates that SSA should "support and complement the full range of broad U.S. national security and foreign assistance objectives."[17] This emphasis of whole-of-government, cross-sectoral awareness is reflected in the creation of a requirement for common interagency SSA strategic planning efforts that take into consideration the full country and regional context—security (including justice and law enforcement), politics, society, and economics—with a view to ensuring greater U.S. government unity of effort. Moreover, the PPD—like the QDDR before it—places a concomitant premium on the importance of monitoring and evaluation as tools for ensuring the effectiveness of SSA. More specifically, it puts in place a "requirement for measurable security sector assistance objectives, appropriate data collection of the impacts and results of security sector assistance programs, and improved efforts to inform decision-making processes with data on what works and what does not work through impact evaluations when permissible."[18] This aspect of the PPD is reflected in the emphasis we place in Chapter Four on developing practical benchmarks (in conjunction with, and with the full participation of, partner nations) for assessing both the effectiveness of

---

[16] The White House, "Presidential Policy Directive 23: Security Sector Assistance," April 5, 2013.

[17] The White House, 2013.

[18] The White House, 2013.

security and justice assistance programs and progress on security sector reform objectives.

From Security Assistance to Security and Justice Sector Partnerships

In light of the research undertaken for this report and our review of current and emerging U.S. national security policy strategies as we have summarized (and in place of the more traditional SSA paradigm), we propose the concept of *security and justice sector partnerships* as a holistic way of thinking about efforts to harness security capacity-building to broader U.S. foreign policy goals, while simultaneously reflecting some of the principles and values contained in the QDDR and PPD as reviewed above. While subsequent chapters will examine the role of security and justice sector (SJS) partnerships (SJSPs) in achieving U.S. strategic objectives in the aftermath of the Arab uprisings, we see the SJSP concept as one that potentially has broad applicability at the global level.

The five chief characteristics of the SJSP concept, as we see them, are:

- **more explicit linkage between military and nonmilitary forms of security assistance** so as to better reflect the interdependence in many settings between civilian law and justice institutions and broader structures of national security more commonly associated with armed forces. This, in turn, needs to be reflected in better interagency planning, coordination, and implementation on the U.S. side, such that SJSP programs run by multiple U.S. government entities serve the common strategic goals generated by the enhanced interagency planning envisaged in the new SSA PPD.

- **an emphasis on building the human capacity** conducive to fostering positive and sustainable change in the norms and operational culture in security institutions.

- where possible and practical, **SJSPs should advance security sector reforms consonant with U.S. reform goals in other, nonsecurity sectors** (e.g., control of corruption, democratic governance) as part of an effort whose ultimate goal is to foster self-sufficiency, good governance, and civilian oversight of national security affairs in partner nations.
- the **purpose, objectives, substance, and evaluation criteria for SJSP programs should be devised in consultation with partner nations** to ensure maximum country ownership and transparency.
- **practical benchmarks for measuring progress in developing security capacity and, where appropriate, in achieving security sector reforms**, should be integrated into SJSPs so that the United States and partner nations will have a common reference point for gauging performance and determining whether and how program implementation needs to be altered. While this approach is most practicable for partnerships that fall within the remit of U.S. foreign assistance, aspects of the model may also be appropriate for certain relationships based primarily on foreign military sales (FMS).

Study Approach

RAND was asked to undertake three distinct tasks. The first was to assess current approaches to U.S. security and justice sector assistance in the MENA region in terms of objectives, processes, stakeholder involvement, resource implications, and outcomes. To this end, we assembled funding data from seven forms of SJS programs active in the region: foreign military financing (FMF); IMET; International Narcotics Control and Law Enforcement; Nonproliferation, Anti-Terrorism, Demining, and Related Programs; Drug Interdiction and Counter-Drug Activities; transfer of excess stock, and the Military Assistance Program. We looked at these data alongside FMS and various indicators of governance to establish a baseline for categorizing and characterizing SJS relationships in the region. This allowed us to look broadly at magnitudes and types of funding in countries with varying governance traits. We then consulted with a broad range of SJS stakeholders including relevant U.S. government entities at the State

Department; other agencies in Washington, D.C. (Office of the Secretary of Defense, USAID, MCC); and video teleconference and telephone consultation with U.S. embassies in Saudi Arabia, the United Arab Emirates, Yemen, and Morocco. Regional travel involved meetings with U.S. country teams in Egypt and Bahrain, Bahraini officials, and nongovernmental organizations. Finally, consultation with the British Foreign and Commonwealth Office and the Ministry of Defence in London, as well as the British embassy in Bahrain, permitted us to learn more about how a close U.S. ally and another provider of significant levels of security assistance to the region approach some of these same questions.

Using the research and findings from the first task, we set out in our second task: to develop new models for security and justice sector partnerships that would improve the integration of security and reform objectives. We initially developed three hypothetical models to organize our thinking—"encouragement," "security sector benchmarks," and "cross-sector benchmarks"—with each representing varying levels of emphasis on reforms and benchmarking criteria. As our analysis of the data and findings from our interviews and consultations progressed, however, we opted to propose a single, enhanced-planning approach that would draw on the most practical aspects of all three models while maintaining sufficient flexibility for tailoring the approach to specific country nuances and needs.

Our third and final task was to translate these models into concrete and actionable options for the State Department as it undertakes strategic planning for SJSPs in the wake of the Arab uprisings and in light of emerging policy frameworks and guidance.

Organization of the Report

Chapter Two presents our analysis of current SSA programs in the MENA region, looking at program mechanics, funding types, and the governance characteristics of various countries. From this research we are able to draw some conclusions about broad patterns regarding types of security cooperation (assistance recipients vs. cash customers), the balance between different types of assistance (security assistance vs. economic aid), regime types, and state fragility in the MENA countries where the United States runs security assistance programs.

Chapter Three presents the broad findings of our interviews and stakeholder consultations with respect to how those currently involved in SJS assistance view the purposes, implementation, and effectiveness of these programs. We then move on to a discussion of how these findings might inform new approaches to SJSPs in light of regional transformations and opportunities for dialogue created by new global guidance on SSA efforts. In particular, we draw on some of the aspects of SSA that implementers feel have been most effective and discuss how SJSP tools might be refined and enhanced in the future while bearing in mind both new regional challenges as well as realities in the Washington, D.C., policy process. Here, we identify and draw on best practices developed by actors such as the Bureau of International Narcotics and Law Enforcement Affairs, MCC, and USAID, and discuss how aspects of their work might inform the development of an enhanced-planning SJSP model going forward.

Chapter Four contains specific recommendations regarding priority issues, key target countries, relevant benchmarks, and relevant non-MENA experiences for policymakers to consider integrating into their security sector programs in the Middle East.

We should make clear that this report is not designed to be a comprehensive assessment, analysis, or set of recommendations for reforming MENA security sector partnerships in broad terms. We are not asking questions about whether, for example, the provision of specific pieces of equipment to particular countries is consonant with their security needs. Rather, our work here represents a focused effort to assess the implications of the intersection between regional political events, the new strategic realities they create, and ongoing efforts in policy spaces to rethink the logic and norms that underpin U.S. foreign policy generally and security assistance more specifically. It is our hope that this report and the framework it provides will make a modest contribution toward assisting those charged with designing and implementing security assistance programs to begin thinking about some practical ways to adapt their approaches to rapidly changing regional and policy environments.

CHAPTER TWO

What We Know About U.S. Partnerships and Partner Characteristics

U.S. partnership efforts with MENA countries are as complex and diverse as the region itself. As discussed in Chapter One, major changes have been under way in recent years in the U.S. approach to SSA and other forms of partnership around the world. Simultaneous to these changes, seismic shifts have been under way in the political and security environments across the MENA region. In order to develop our framework for SJSPs, we begin with a look at data related to U.S. SSA and engagement over the past nine years, and then more specifically at changes since the start of the Arab uprisings. We then examine the characteristics of MENA countries, focusing on commonly used indicators of state fragility and other measures of governance. We assembled the data not to identify correlations between U.S. assistance and changes in the MENA region—something that would be outside the scope of this report—but rather to serve as a foundation for understanding the nuances of U.S. assistance and the challenges of U.S. engagement in this region.

U.S. Partnerships Defy Simple Descriptions

U.S. SJS partnerships in the MENA region are sometimes oversimplified as two departments—the State Department and the Department of Defense—engaging with wealthier partners through FMS and poorer partners through FMF. While the State and Defense departments oversee the majority of programs that help shape relationships in MENA, myriad U.S. departments and agencies are active across the region, including USAID and the departments of Homeland Security, Justice, Treasury, and Energy. In addition to FMS and FMF, there are dozens of programs guiding SJSPs in areas such as counterterrorism, air and missile defense, maritime security, counternarcotics, and judicial reform. For our analysis, we focused on FMS and U.S. assistance data drawn from USAID's Overseas Loans and Grants reporting, which reports on the main SJS programs driving U.S. foreign assistance: FMF; IMET; International Narcotics Control and Law Enforcement; Nonproliferation, Anti-Terrorism, Demining, and Related Programs; Drug Interdiction and Counter-Drug Activities; transfer of excess stock, and the Military Assistance Program.

A closer look at the data reveals a complex dynamic between FMS and FMF in most MENA countries. As shown in Figure 2.1, every recipient of FMF is also an FMS customer for the United States. In fact, most MENA partners spend more in FMS than FMF, thereby making them important cash customers, not simply eager-to-please grant recipients. Of all MENA partners, only Israel, Yemen, and Tunisia have received more FMF than they have spent through FMS since 2004. Finally, whereas there have been several partners with large FMS contracts (Egypt, Saudi Arabia, the United Arab Emirates, Jordan, and Kuwait), only three—Egypt, Israel, and Jordan—have been major peacetime FMF recipients.

One might argue that U.S. leverage—and ability to push for SJS reform—would be greatest for those partners receiving high levels of FMF and spending little through FMS. This argument rests on the assumption that providing funding creates leverage, while benefiting from a partner's FMS purchases of U.S. equipment and services reduces leverage. Moreover, the argument assumes that whatever leverage exists could be applied to reform without affecting potentially competing U.S. interests. However, these assumptions are not so clear, particularly in the MENA region. Table 2.1 shows that Israel, Egypt, Iraq, and Jordan dominate FMF assistance overall, as well as when accounting for population, gross domestic product (GDP), and FMF as a percentage of military expenditures. In addition to their purchases of FMS discussed above, each of these countries is critically important in advancing regional stability, counterterrorism, and other U.S. objectives, thus

Figure 2.1
Total FMS/FMF Spending, 2004–2012

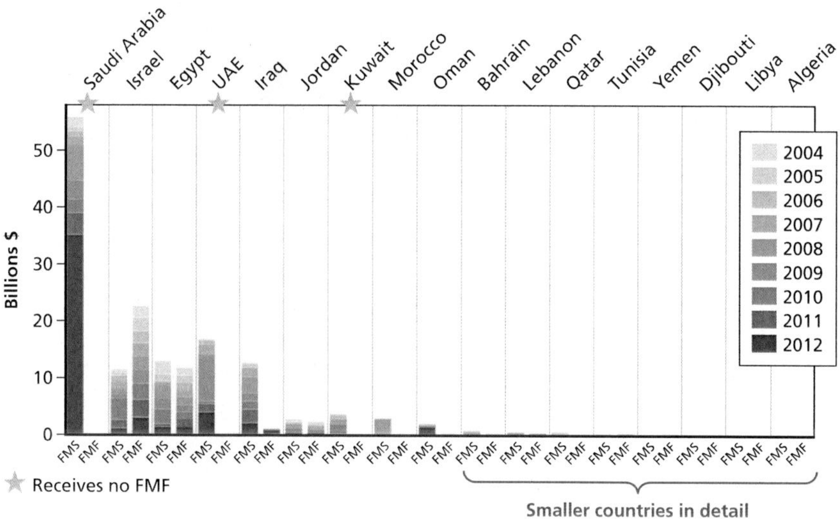

NOTE: These two charts show the vast magnitude in differences between MENA countries (billions vs. millions) in FMF and FMS. Color shadings indicate the year. For Saudi Arabia, the bulk of the FMS was in 2012, with $35 billion in FMS. Some countries are very consistent in FMS per year, such as Egypt. Other countries, like Israel, are getting almost two times more FMF than they are spending in FMS. On the smaller end of the scale, wealthier nations, such as Bahrain and Qatar, receive little or no FMF but purchase actively through FMS. Recently, Lebanon has been purchasing more through FMS than it has been receiving in FMF assistance.

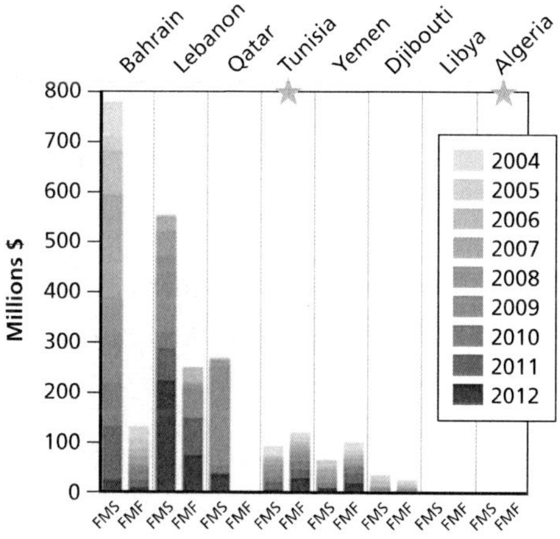

SOURCE: Defense Security Cooperation Agency, *Foreign Military Sales, Foreign Military Construction Sales, and Other Security Cooperation Historical Facts*, September 30, 2012.
RAND *RR605-2.1*

Table 2.1
FMF Averages, by Per Capita, Percentage of GDP, and Percentage of Military Expenditure, 2004–2012

Country	FMF ($K) Average (2004–2012)	Country	FMF Average ($) Per Capita	Country	FMF Average as Percentage of GDP Average	Country	FMF Average as Percentage of Military Expenditures Average
Israel	2,505,695	Israel	88.58	Israel	1.37	*Egypt*	33.77
Egypt	1,295,089	Jordan	80.59	Jordan	1.25	Iraq	29.49
Iraq	850,000	Iraq	26.09	*Egypt*	0.79	Jordan	24.10
Jordan	261,969	*Egypt*	16.04	Iraq	0.78	Israel	19.27
Lebanon	41,576	*Yemen*	8.66	Djibouti	0.42	Djibouti	7.46
Bahrain	14,505	Lebanon	4.52	Lebanon	0.14	*Yemen*	6.70
Tunisia	13,556	*Bahrain*	3.28	*Bahrain*	0.07	Lebanon	3.19
Oman	12,623	Morocco	2.77	*Yemen*	0.05	*Tunisia*	2.46
Yemen	11,409	Oman	1.17	*Tunisia*	0.03	*Bahrain*	2.20
Morocco	9,189	*Tunisia*	0.42	Oman	0.03	Morocco	0.34
Djibouti	3,132	Djibouti	0.13	Morocco	0.01	Oman	0.29
Libya	150	*Libya*	0.00	*Libya*	0.00	*Libya*	0.02

SOURCES: Defense Security Cooperation Agency, 2012; World Bank, *GDP*, web page, undated; World Bank, *Military Expenditures*, web page, undated.
NOTE: Algeria, Iran, Kuwait, Qatar, Saudi Arabia, Syria, United Arab Emirates, and the West Bank and Gaza all receive zero FMF. Italicized countries are most affected by the Arab uprisings.

potentially limiting U.S. willingness to use FMF as leverage to pressure partners into SJS and political reform. In the second tier of recipients, Djibouti and Yemen stand out somewhat when looking at FMF relative to population, GDP, and military expenditure. Both play vital roles in U.S. counterterrorism efforts, however, thus complicating FMF as a lever for reform. In fact, no matter how FMF is considered, no country stands out as a "high FMF leverage" prospect, including those most affected by the Arab uprisings (indicated by italics). Figure 2.2 depicts the per capita distribution of FMS and FMF graphically, showing that only Israel and Yemen receive significantly more FMF than they spend on FMS, and Israel still spends large amounts on FMS.

The United States faces a leverage dilemma even with those countries that receive large amounts of FMF (i.e., Egypt, Jordan). High

Figure 2.2
Average FMF vs. FMS Per Capita, 2004–2012

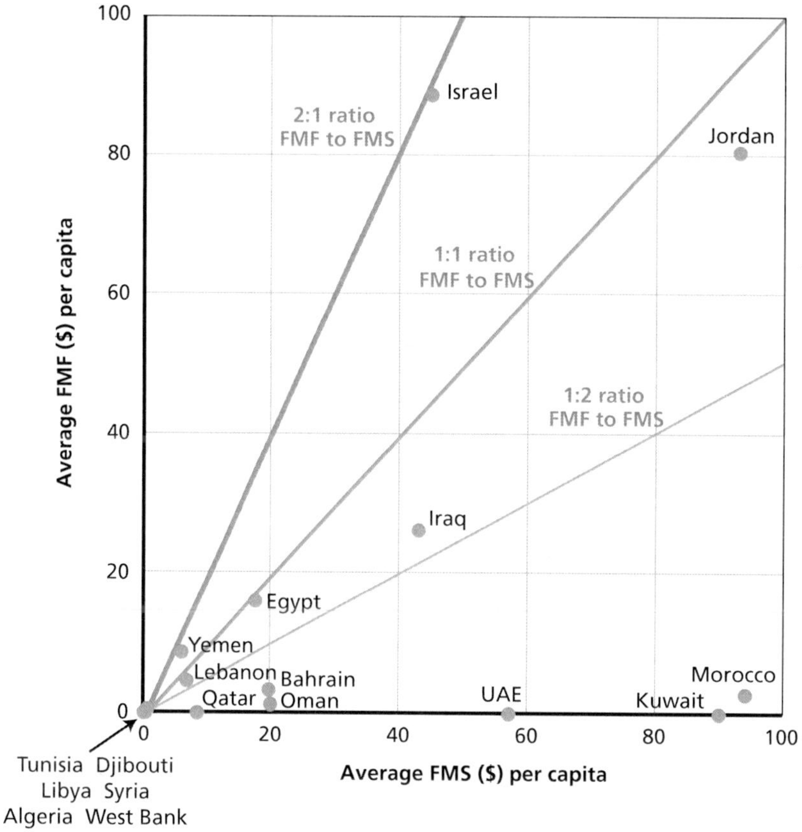

SOURCE: Defense Security Cooperation Agency, 2012.
NOTE: This chart illustrates the dominance of Israel and Jordan in terms of FMF and FMS per capita. Many countries receive little to no FMF, such as Kuwait, the United Arab Emirates, and Qatar. Others, like Tunisia and Djibouti, have some FMF and FMS, but per capita amounts are so small compared with Israel and Jordan that they appear close to zero on the graph. Saudi Arabia is excluded, as it is an FMS outlier at $736 per capita with $0 FMF.
RAND *RR605-2.2*

levels of FMF are not primarily provided to encourage reform, but rather to advance other U.S. interests in the region. In other words, the United States likely needs these partners at least as much as they need the United States. A recent Army War College report explains the challenges in making assumptions about leverage, using aid to Egypt as an example: "Many political figures in the United States consider the aid to be a form of leverage over Egypt and believe it entitles the United States to expect certain norms of behavior from the Egyptian government. From the Egyptian perspective, the aid is the least the United States can do to reward Egypt for all it does strategically and politically for the United States in the region."[1]

Although there is very little research on the ability of SJS assistance to provide leverage, there has been extensive analysis on the ability of U.S. and international development aid to influence partner nations. While some research has found that aid, on average, can have a positive impact on government policies, others have found little evidence of such leverage.[2] While not without its own controversies, there is generally more agreement that aid is more effective in those countries with stronger governance mechanisms, one of the underlying principles behind the U.S. Millennium Challenge Account.[3]

While the evidence is mixed as to whether aid provides leverage,[4] every official we interviewed argued that FMS and SJS assistance are important components of U.S. relationships in the region. While partners can purchase military equipment and services from providers like Russia and China, the reality is that many MENA partners perceive U.S. equipment and support as the best in the world and value

---

[1] Gregory Aftandilian, *Egypt's New Regime and the Future of the U.S.-Egyptian Strategic Relationship*, Carlisle Barracks, Pa.: Strategic Studies Institute, U.S. Army War College Press, April 2013, p. 5.

[2] For an excellent overview of this debate, see Andrew Mold, *Policy Ownership and Aid Conditionality in the Light of the Financial Crisis: A Critical Review*, Development Centre Studies, OECD Publications, 2009, pp. 43–45.

[3] Paul Collier, "Is Aid Oil? An Analysis of Whether Africa Can Absorb More Aid," *World Development*, Vol. 34, No. 9, 2006, p. 1488.

[4] Mold, 2009.

their relationships with the U.S. military. While partners receiving SJS assistance could threaten to stop supporting U.S. counterterrorism, access, and other objectives and rely on other governments for support, MENA partners do not use a purely transactional calculus. These partners value not just U.S. funds and equipment, but also the relationships themselves, which are strengthened through these programs. For example, U.S. country team officials in two Gulf countries provided examples of how their host nation counterparts frequently express their appreciation of both U.S. equipment and training. As one interviewee noted: "They take every [Professional Military Education] slot we can provide them."[5] Thus, while U.S. leverage is limited, so is partner leverage.

The relationships are truly two-way streets. Far from being mere transactions, SJS cooperation is profoundly relationship-based, with deep historical roots, personal connections, sometimes baffling complexity, and multiple dimensions. For example, a U.S. official in one country explained that the focus is on working with "constructive people, all of whom have benefited in the past from U.S. training." Another U.S. official in that country said, "Below the very top level, there is a large cadre of officers eager to strengthen partnerships. That's who the U.S. is betting on." Another official noted that these relationships sometimes became stronger than those within the host nation itself, saying, "They won't share intelligence [on drug trafficking] with each other, but they share with the U.S., and then we share with their colleagues from other offices."[6]

Finally, as shown in Figures 2.3 and 2.4, FMS and SJS assistance are only part of the story and not always the most significant part. While our analysis focused on MENA security and justice sectors, the data show the crucial role of other U.S. assistance in strengthening partners and U.S. relationships with them. The figures also provide an interesting perspective on relative levels of assistance and show whether assistance levels have been increasing or decreasing. For example, while

---

5 Nonattribution interviews with U.S. officials in the Middle East, Spring 2013.

6 Nonattribution interviews with U.S. officials in a MENA country, Spring 2013.

Figure 2.3
Total U.S. Foreign Assistance to MENA, 2006–2014

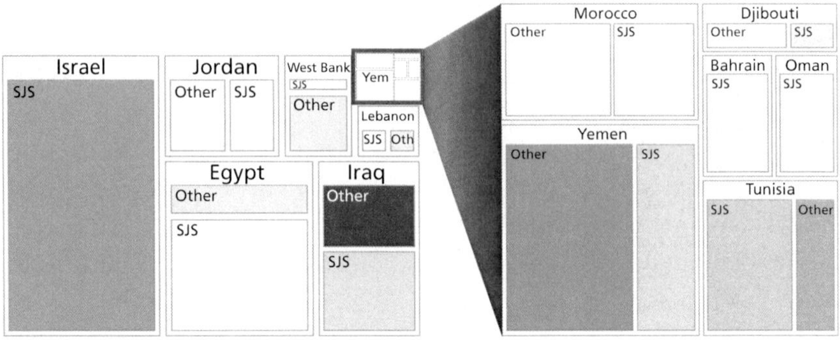

SOURCE: www.ForeignAssistance.gov.
NOTES: "Other" refers to all other U.S. Foreign Assistance—economic, human rights, health, etc. This tree map displays relative proportions of U.S. assistance to MENA countries. Blue shades indicate upward trends in assistance levels from 2006 to 2014 (including programmatic planning), red indicates downward trends, and white is steady. Israel dominates all U.S. foreign assistance (all SJS) and showed an upward trend. Jordan, Egypt, Iraq, and West Bank/Gaza dominated the rest of U.S. foreign assistance. With the smaller beneficiaries, Lebanon is on a downward trend with Yemen and Tunisia showing an upward trend. Of note, Jordan and Yemen received more in "other" assistance than SJS.
RAND *RR605-2.3*

Jordan receives the most FMF per capita, it receives even more from the United States in economic development assistance.

Moreover, each of these countries has a unique history regarding the rationale and impact of this assistance. For example, Jordan's security forces have trained Iraqi and Palestinian forces in Jordan. It operates the Peace Operations Training Center and the King Abdullah Special Operations Training Center, important vehicles for promoting regional cooperation. Jordan has also played an important role in supporting peace with Israel, signing a peace treaty in 1994 and a trade treaty in 1996. Lacking the resources of its Persian Gulf neighbors, however, Jordan receives more development aid than SJS assistance. On the other hand, given its greater wealth compared to Jordan, Bahrain only receives SJS assistance. This assistance is at relatively low levels compared to Jordan but relatively high compared with other Gulf countries. SJS assistance is seen as a helpful means by which the

Figure 2.4
Total U.S. Foreign Assistance to MENA by Region, 2006–2014

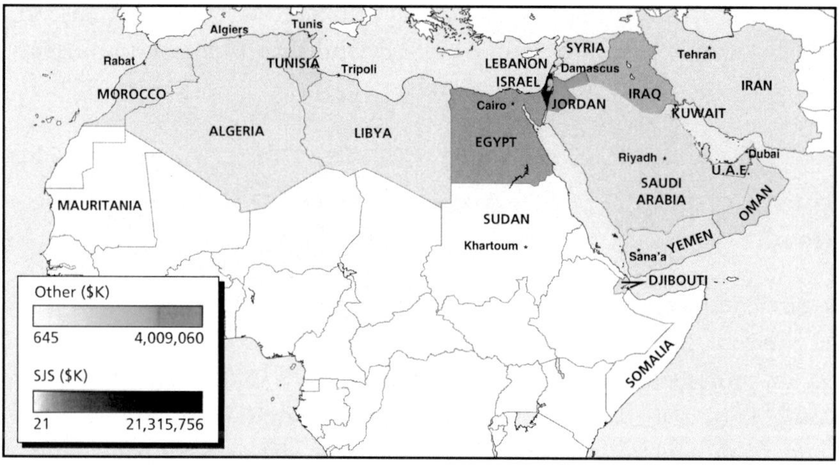

SOURCE: www.ForeignAssistance.gov.
NOTES: "Other" refers to all other U.S. foreign assistance—economic, human rights, health, etc. From a geographic perspective, the map depicts the degree of "other" vs. SJS assistance planned for 2014. Israel and Egypt dominate in SJS assistance, while Jordan is predominantly in the "other" category.
RAND *RR605-2.4*

United States can engage the Bahraini government in regional deterrence activities (including through FMF); counterterrorism training (including through Section 1206 Train and Equip Program funding); and in professional military education (through the IMET program).

Although outside the scope of this report, it is important to note that other factors—such as U.S. objectives relating to diplomatic support; regional peace and stability; and military access to bases, airspace, and the Suez Canal—also play critical roles in shaping U.S. partnerships in the region.

As the data show, there is great variety in the levels and distribution of FMS, SJS assistance, and economic assistance, which makes it challenging to gauge how effective these tools might be in shaping relationships in the MENA region. Our interviews, meanwhile, revealed the complexity and uniqueness of every relationship in the region, highlighting the need for sophisticated, proactive, and flexible partnership models. Different partners play important roles advancing particular bilateral and regional security goals—for example, Saudi Arabia and the United Arab Emirates in deterring potential regional adversaries; Yemen, Algeria, and Libya in counterterrorism; Jordan and Morocco in strengthening regional stability; and Egypt in most of these areas as well as Suez Canal transit.

Adjustments in U.S. SJS Approaches Have Been Slow and Uneven

As discussed in Chapter One, guidance from the U.S. President and Secretary of State has changed since 2010 in two important areas: (1) U.S. promotion of democratic and SJS reform in the MENA region, and (2) U.S. approaches to SJS globally. U.S. diplomatic and military engagement generally changes gradually, and changes are particularly challenging when the political and security landscape is in constant flux. Nevertheless, a look at the data from 2006 to 2014 (including programmatic planning) provides some valuable insights into how the United States is adjusting its approaches to SJS in the MENA region.

Table 2.2 examines some of the countries that experienced the Arab uprisings most intensively, and thus where one would expect change in foreign assistance as a result of the unrest. Of the seven countries, Yemen, Tunisia, and Libya experienced an increase in assistance averaged from 2013 to 2014 (planned), the first years where policy might logically change assistance levels as a result of events. This is notable considering that overall U.S. foreign assistance reached a peak in 2010 at 36 billion dollars, a 74-percent increase from 2006 levels, and the countries affected by the Arab uprisings reached a combined peak in 2012. After 2012, both overall U.S. foreign assistance and assistance to countries affected by the Arab uprisings decreased as budget constraints began to take effect. Bahrain, Egypt, Tunisia, and Libya all received more SJS, while Jordan, Yemen, and Morocco received more "other" funding.

To hone in on specific details:

Table 2.2
All MENA Foreign Assistance 2006–2014: Trends and Comparisons

Sum of Amount ($K) Country	Avg ($K) (2006–2012)	Avg ($K) (2013–2014)		Avg ($K) (2006–2014) % of Cat	Trend (2006–2014) Vert is 2012
Egypt	**1,666,138**	1,623,654	⇩	**1,656,697**	
Security and Justice Sector	1,301,439	1,276,823	⇩	78%	
Other (Econ, Dem, Human Rights, etc.)	364,698	346,832	⇩	22%	
Jordan	**736,493**	**705,233**	⇩	**729,547**	
Security and Justice Sector	320,531	303,469	⇩	43%	
Other (Econ, Dem, Human Rights, etc.)	415,962	401,765	⇩	57%	
Yemen	**57,523**	**73,595**	⇧	**61,095**	
Security and Justice Sector	16,623	28,076	⇧	31%	
Other (Econ, Dem, Human Rights, etc.)	40,900	45,520	⇧	69%	
Morocco	**33,245**	**31,814**	⇩	**32,927**	
Security and Justice Sector	14,137	13,856	⇩	43%	
Other (Econ, Dem, Human Rights, etc.)	19,108	17,958	⇩	57%	
Tunisia	**26,321**	**54,004**	⇧	**32,472**	
Security and Justice Sector	19,963	29,771	⇧	68%	
Other (Econ, Dem, Human Rights, etc.)	6,357	24,233	⇧	32%	
Bahrain	**14,116**	**12,433**	⇩	**13,742**	
Security and Justice Sector	14,116	12,433	⇩	100%	
Other (Econ, Dem, Human Rights, etc.)	—	—	⇔	0%	
Libya	**2,296**	**4,235**	⇧	**$2,727**	
Security and Justice Sector	1,131	4,000	⇧	65%	
Other (Econ, Dem, Human Rights, etc.)	1,165	235	⇩	35%	
Select MENA Countries 2006–2014	**7,209,372**	**6,720,638**	⇩	**7,100,764**	
All U.S. Foreign Assistance	**29,631,921**	**32,448,976**	⇧	**30,257,933**	

SOURCE: www.foreignassistance.gov

- Bahrain receives strictly SJS funding with a downward trend since 2010.
- Libya has the least amount of foreign assistance provided overall but with a dramatic increase in SJS in 2013–2014. "Other" foreign assistance to Libya decreased significantly and accounts for only 35 percent of U.S. assistance (vs. 65 percent for SJS) from 2006 to 2014.
- Yemen shows a steady increase in foreign assistance through 2012, when it reached its maximum. In 2013–2014, foreign assistance is lower but still well above previous averages. SJS funding percentage is now nearly twice the 2006–2012 average, with a slight increase in "Other" funding.

- Jordan's overall assistance has decreased from a high in 2008. "Other" funding makes up 57 percent of U.S. assistance, compared with 43 percent for SJS.

Variations in MENA Country Characteristics Drive the Need for More Sophisticated Planning

In addition to analyzing variations in U.S. SJS assistance and other aspects of U.S. partnerships with MENA countries, we also sought to gain insights into MENA country characteristics. Every country in the MENA region has its own unique history and unique relationships with the United States. Moreover, as the map in Figure 2.5 shows, the Arab uprisings have had vastly different impacts on the countries in the region.

To examine MENA country characteristics, our group examined a number of different indicators from well-known organizations such as Freedom House, the Center for Systemic Peace, Transparency International, the World Bank, and the Fund for Peace to provide an

Figure 2.5
Map of Arab Uprisings

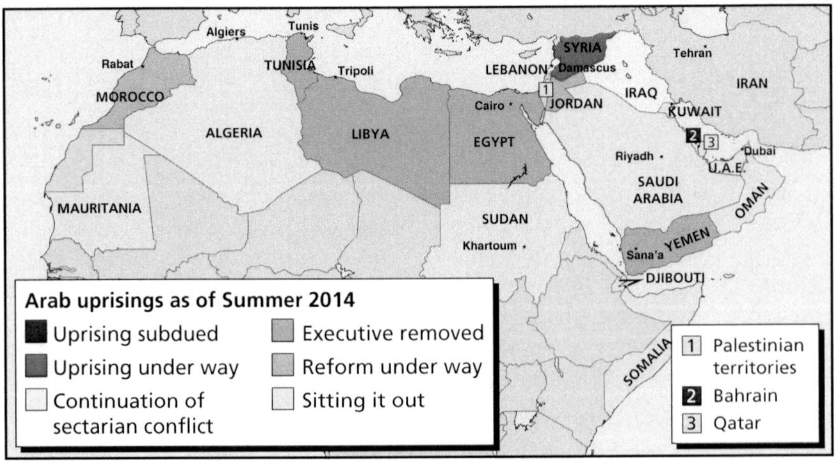

RAND *RR605-2.5*

overall representation of changes in the region over the past few years. However, after comparing all the different types of indexes—each with different scoring ranges and criteria—we chose to focus on just two indexes.

First, we used the Center for Systemic Peace's State Fragility Index (SFI) to rate the level of fragility in MENA countries before and after the first episodes of the Arab uprisings.[7] While there are several academic indexes that evaluate a country's fragility or stability, the SFI is well-respected, has a long history, and was developed to support U.S. government country analysis. It rates most countries in the world on a scale from a least-fragile score of 0 (e.g., Sweden) to a most-fragile score of 25 (e.g., Somalia in 2011), based on four components: security, political, economic, and social. As shown in the example in Figure 2.6, each component is examined in terms of effectiveness and legitimacy.

As with all such indexes, SFI is less a crystal ball than a tool to help analyze and compare the underlying factors of a country's relative strengths and weaknesses. Because indexes such as SFI use lagging indicators, they are most useful to facilitate discussions about general country characteristics rather than as a reflection of recent events.

Figure 2.6
State Fragility Index 2012, Bahrain Example

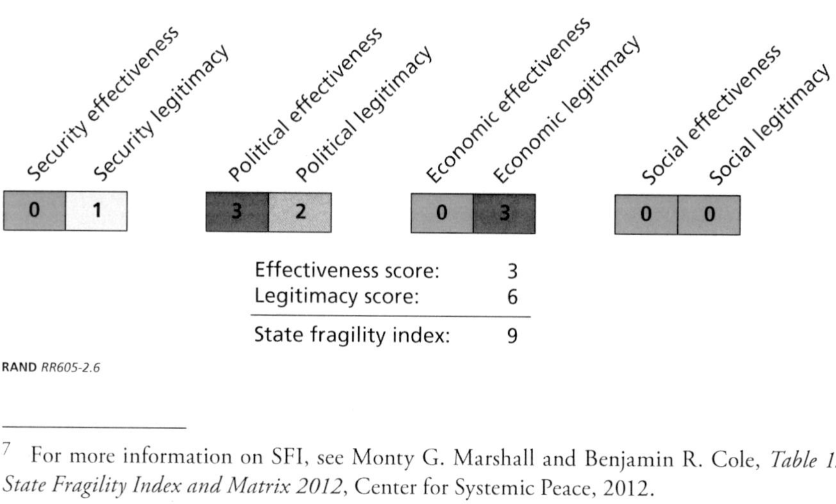

RAND *RR605-2.6*

[7] For more information on SFI, see Monty G. Marshall and Benjamin R. Cole, *Table 1: State Fragility Index and Matrix 2012*, Center for Systemic Peace, 2012.

When looking at SFI scores for 2012, we found fairly wide diversity in estimated levels of fragility.[8] In Table 2.3, we illustrate SFI scores for several MENA countries strongly affected by the Arab uprisings.

In some cases, like Tunisia, Egypt, and Yemen, fragility was assessed as decreasing in 2012 compared with 2009—though the changes in aggregate were not dramatic, given that some indicators (e.g., political legitimacy) may have improved while others (e.g., security effectiveness) may have declined. Fragility in Bahrain and Libya, on the other hand, was assessed as dramatically increasing. It is also interesting to compare the countries with each other. Egypt, for example, was assessed as far more fragile than Bahrain in 2009, but by 2012 the two countries were not that far apart—though one might argue that Bahrain at its most fragile was still in better shape than Egypt, and far better than Yemen despite their signs of slight improvements as of early 2012. Finally, a comparison of Tunisia and Libya illustrates how two countries can take dramatically different paths, reinforcing the need for sophisticated, agile, foreign assistance planning.

For our second measure of country characteristics, we chose the Failed States Index (FSI) from the Fund for Peace.[9] The FSI also includes the most meaningful political-military dimensions that U.S.

Table 2.3
SFI Scores for Select MENA Countries

Select MENA Countries	2009 SFI Score	2012 SFI Score	Fragility
Libya	7	16	+9 (Worse)
Bahrain	4	9	+5 (Worse)
Yemen	18	17	–1 (Better)
Egypt	13	11	–2 (Better)
Tunisia	7	5	–2 (Better)

8 Marshall and Cole, 2012.

9 Fund For Peace, *Failed States Index*, web page, undated.

security and justice sector assistance (SJSA) would most directly affect: rule of law, human rights, corruption, flawed elections, internal conflict, policing, foreign assistance, etc.

Each FSI indicator ranges from 0 to 10, with 10 being the worst possible score. Each country was grouped by State Department Bureau region and then aggregated over time. These scores provide a snapshot of each geographic region from a political-military, social, and economic perspective. This high level of aggregation means that even small changes may indicate significant shifts by individual countries.

Figure 2.7 displays an aggregate score of all six FSI political-military indicators from 2006 to 2012, broken down by geographic region, with the dashed line representing post-Arab uprisings. Based on these scores, we see a clear worsening in political-military scores in the run-up to the start of the Arab uprisings. Though not displayed, the Near East Asia region (including MENA countries) was the worst of all regions in 2012 in the political-military subdimension of human rights/rule of law. Our models showed similar deteriorations relative to the rest of the world (which generally saw modest improvements)

Figure 2.7
Failed States Index—Political-Military Indicators, 2006–2012

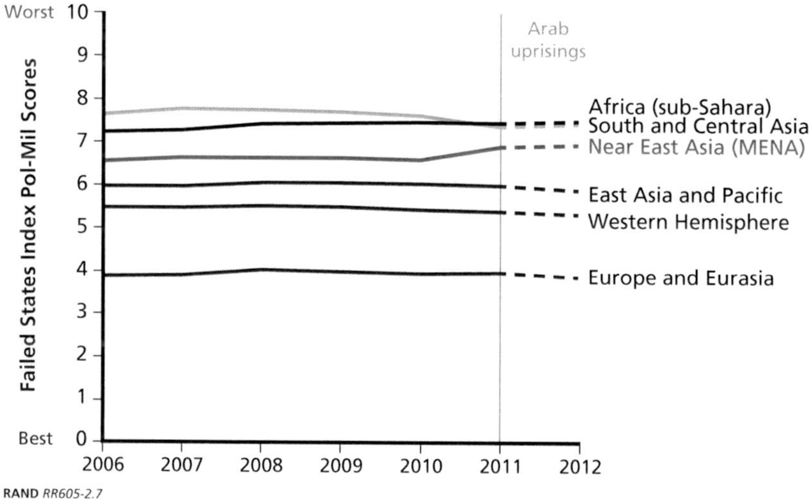

RAND *RR605-2.7*

in areas such as group grievances and poverty. For example, MENA countries as a group scored better than Western Hemisphere and East Asia countries in the FSI's Poverty subdimension in 2010, but not in 2012.

Figure 2.8 shows SJS assistance from 2006 to 2014 (including 2014 planned data), broken down by geographic region, with dashed lines representing post-Arab uprisings. The log10 scale is used to account for the wide range of assistance levels. What is clear is that the Near East Asia (MENA) countries consistently receive high levels of funding with relatively little variation. South and Central Asia saw a large increase with the surge to fund Afghanistan and Pakistan—but by 2014, SJSA declines below 2006 levels, reflecting the drawdown from Afghanistan. Western Hemisphere Affairs and Europe and Eurasia also show steady decreases and by 2014 will be below 2006 levels. Africa continues an up-and-down SJSA trend. East Asia Pacific (has received the least amount of funding but is showing a steady uptick in SJSA since 2011.

Figure 2.8
Security and Justice Sector Assistance, by Region, 2006–2014

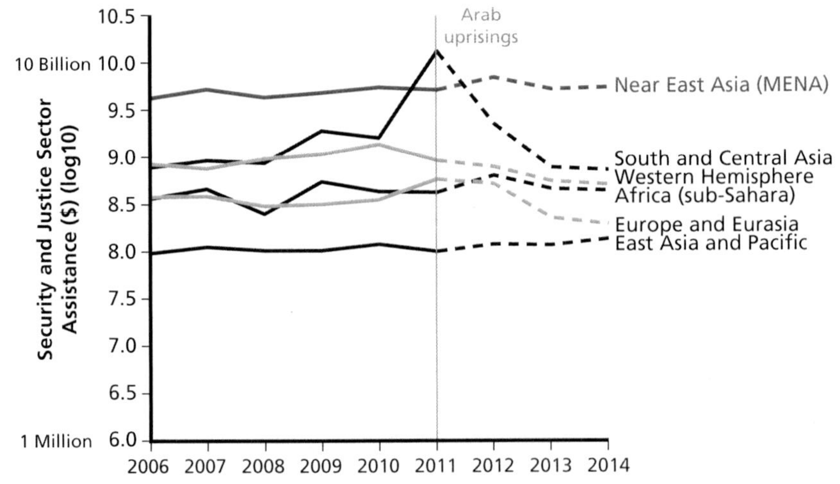

RAND *RR605-2.8*

Figure 2.9 examines FSI political-military indicators (2006–2012) and SJSA (2006–2014) in select MENA countries that experienced turmoil related to the Arab uprisings. Egypt receives the most SJSA by far, with nearly a straight-line trend since 2006. Since 2010, Egypt's FSI political-military scores have worsened, and are expected to decline further for 2013. Tunisia's assistance has increased steadily since 2006, with a peak in 2012. Its FSI political-military scores worsened significantly since 2009, but Tunisia continues to score better than the region as a whole. Yemen has also seen a steady increase in SJSA, but what stands out most is that of the five countries, Yemen started with the worst FSI political-military scores and continued to worsen through 2012. Bahrain's SJSA has seen a slight decrease since 2006. Its FSI political-military scores have worsened significantly since 2010, but Bahrain still has the best FSI political-military score of the five in 2012. For Libya, SJSA increased significantly after 2010. Its FSI political-military scores have worsened significantly since 2010. Libya's SJSA has decreased but is still much higher than in 2006.

In this chapter, we've examined the differences in the nature of U.S. SJS and other programs, as well as differences in country characteristics among MENA countries. We've also examined how SJSA and measures of stability and governance have changed since the start of the Arab uprisings. Looking back at SFI scores, it is clear that fragility in the MENA region is extremely difficult to predict or affect. And when looking at the data throughout this chapter—particularly Tables 2.1, 2.2, and 2.3 and Figures 2.6, 2.7, 2.8, and 2.9—we see few clear relationships among U.S. assistance, MENA country characteristics, and outcomes as measured against U.S. reform objectives.

As we shall examine in greater detail in Chapter Three, it is clear that the complexities of the region present significant challenges for improving SJS partnerships and promoting reform. New partnership models will require sophisticated approaches to planning that involve nuanced assessments of each U.S. program and how it supports reform and other objectives, as well as assessments of MENA country characteristics and how to adapt to fast-moving changes.

Figure 2.9
Select MENA Countries: Failed States Index Political-Military Scores, 2006–2012; Security and Justice Sector Assistance (SJSA) ($), 2006–2014

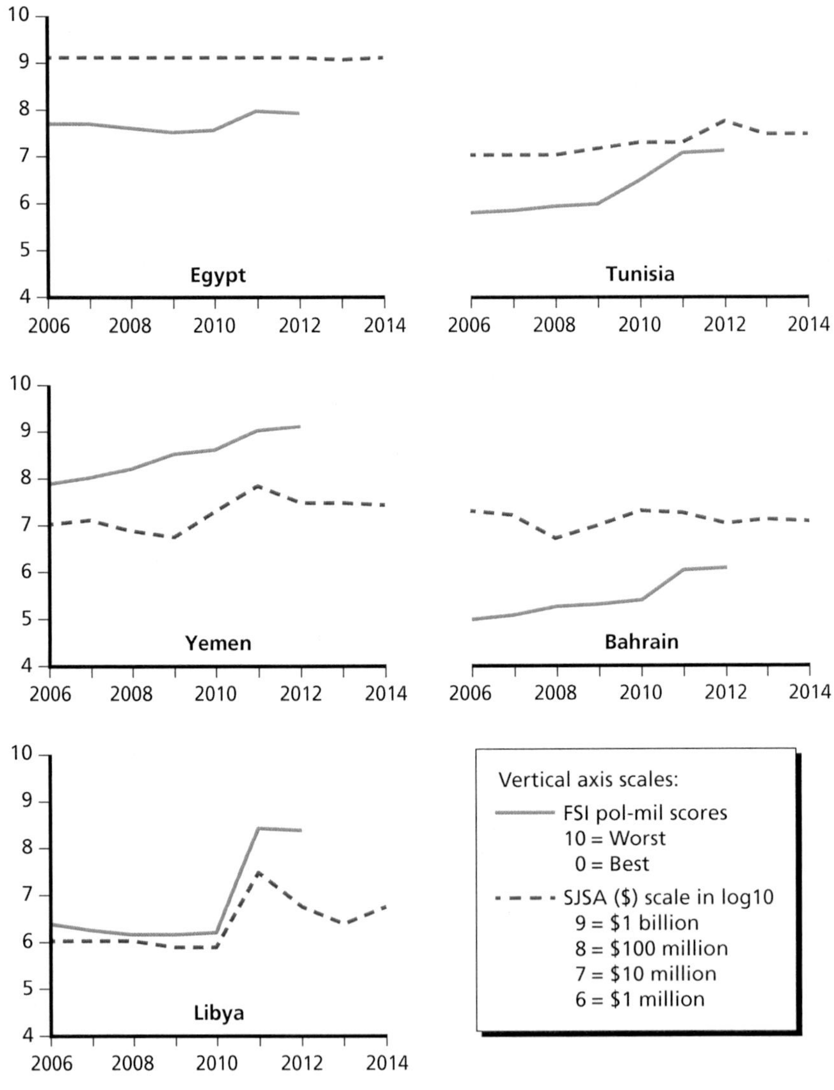

RAND *RR605-2.9*

CHAPTER THREE

Applying New Partnership Models

This chapter presents the key findings of our research, which are mainly based on interviews and stakeholder consultations with respect to how they view the purposes, implementation, and effectiveness of SJS assistance and programs. The chapter begins with a discussion of the three models we originally employed to test our hypothesis, namely, that the State Department could utilize one or more templates to improve the effectiveness of SJS assistance and promote reform, particularly in the MENA region. Next, we present a consolidated, hybrid model as a way forward. We then move on to a discussion of how our research findings might inform new approaches to SJSPs in light of regional transformations and opportunities for dialogue created by new global guidance on SSA. We present the discussion in terms of opportunities, challenges, and best practices. In particular, we draw on some of the aspects of SSA that implementers believe have been most effective, and we discuss how SJSP tools might be refined and enhanced in the future.

The Original Three Partnership Models

We initially developed three hypothetical partnership models as a way to help organize our thinking—"encouragement," "SJS reform benchmarks," and "U.S. governmentwide (cross-sector) benchmarks"—with each representing varying levels of emphasis on reforms and assessment criteria. The general idea was to flesh out the defining characteristics and associated actions for each model, and then try to classify MENA countries according to regime type and overall partnership with the

United States (i.e., U.S. leverage and prioritization). The two key questions we ended up considering in this process were:

- In terms of U.S. leverage, to what extent does the partner rely on U.S. assistance? What does the balance of U.S.-provided security, justice, and development assistance look like?
- In terms of prioritization, how important is the partner to U.S. national security and regional objectives?

Each model is discussed briefly below, followed by a discussion of our consolidated model.

Encouragement Model

Our encouragement model was intended for countries over which the United States has minimal leverage (e.g., "cash customer" partners), yet are important to achieving U.S. objectives. In this kind of model, security cooperation activities and assistance would be linked more directly and explicitly to achieving both U.S. and partner interests than is typically the case. In some instances, breaking the usual norm, the United States may even choose to pay for wealthy countries to participate in specific types of security cooperation activities in an effort to bolster the partner country's interest in, and awareness of, an area that is more firmly in the interest of the United States. Examples could include expanding human rights–related training for junior officers, handling of forensic evidence during an investigation, and a host of issues related to supporting the development of civil society and civil-military relations. In the encouragement model, reform goals are broad and have no explicit benchmarks for measuring progress along the way, nor are there any repercussions for failing to make progress. Moreover, nonbinding memoranda of understanding (MOUs) are established, which could be applied to the SJS sector as a whole, or to specific cases and/or programs of assistance. Ideally, the MOUs would incorporate SMART (specific, measurable, attainable, results-oriented, and time-bound) objectives, and both performance (i.e., outputs) and effectiveness (i.e., outcomes) metrics that would allow progress to be tracked over time. The United States would not dictate the specific objectives, but would rather remain in a consulting role with the partner country as objectives are developed and prioritized, indirectly helping to shape the plan as it evolves. The intention is not for the United States to "punish" the partner when objectives are not being met or falling short of specific milestones, but to demonstrate the intrinsic value in conducting regular assessments, documenting progress, ensuring the partner takes ownership of the assessment, and assisting the partner in the prioritization of key objectives.

SJS Reform Benchmarks Model (Limited to SJS Sector)

Our SJS reform benchmarks model was intended for countries over which the United States has considerable leverage, particularly countries that rely on U.S. SJSA, and are not as high a priority to achieving U.S. objectives as those countries that would fit in the encouragement model. In this type of model, security cooperation activities are more clearly linked to U.S. and partner interests than is currently the case (as in the encouragement model), and the United States may again consider paying even for wealthy countries to participate in specific security cooperation activities that are more firmly in the bounds of U.S. interests. One difference between this model and the encouragement model is that equipment sales would be embedded in comprehensive SJS reform planning, resourcing, and assessments. Another difference would be the introduction of memoranda of agreement (MOAs)—which, unlike MOUs, would be binding. The United Kingdom has used this type of approach with partner countries in the area of counterterrorism training, for example, whereby progress is assessed against specific benchmarks that both countries agreed to. The idea is that if insufficient progress has been made, the training would cease. In practice, however, because the strategy is agreed to by both sides, realistic benchmarks are established and partners make measurable progress, so training is rarely stopped. The terms of the MOAs would apply to SJS only. As in the encouragement model, SMART objectives and associated metrics would be included in the MOAs, and directly linked to resource allocation. Policy waivers would be permissible. USAID provides a useful model for developing host country–based objectives tied to resource allocations through its Country Development Cooperation Strategies.[1]

U.S. Governmentwide Benchmarks Model (Cross-Sector)

Our U.S. governmentwide benchmarks model was intended for countries over which the United States had maximum leverage, particularly those that rely extensively on both SJS and economic assistance, and which are less critical to achieving U.S. objectives than those in the encouragement model. This model is similar to the SJS benchmarks model, with two notable exceptions. First, equipment sales/SJS assistance would be embedded in comprehensive *governance* (not just SJS) reform planning, resourcing, and assessments. Second, the MOA would apply to all sectors—SJS and also economic—which would necessitate a very tight U.S. governmentwide approach. Table 3.1 summarizes the characteristics discussed in this section as they apply to each type of partnership model.

Table 3.1
Characteristics Associated with Partnership Models

	Model Type		
Model Characteristics	**Encouragement**	**SJS Benchmarks**	**Cross-Sector Benchmarks**
Joint metrics	X	X	X
Equipment sales linked to SJS benchmarks		X	
Equipment sales linked to cross-sector benchmarks			X
Flexible MOUs	X		
Binding MOAs apply to SJS sector		X	
Binding MOAs apply to all sectors		X	X
Waiver possible		X	X
Degree of leverage	Low	Medium	High
Criticality of U.S. interests	High	Medium	Low

1 USAID, ADS Chapter 200, "Introduction to Programming Policy," February 10, 2012a, pp. 22–32.

Change of Approach to a Consolidated "Enhanced Partnership Planning Model"

Originally, our approach to this report followed a sort of quid-pro-quo mentality—specifically, that the United States should use its assistance as leverage to encourage further reforms wherever feasible. As our interviews and consultations progressed in Washington, D.C., and in the field, we received feedback on the models indicating that it would be difficult in practice to determine which countries should be in each model, and that any actions beyond those associated with the less-intrusive encouragement model would be politically unacceptable to the partner and thus very difficult to implement. One interviewee in Washington gave several examples of partners whose reactions to U.S. pressures proved difficult to predict. U.S. efforts to identify "red lines"—the point at which a partner might walk away from the relationship—were unsuccessful. While our initial assumption was that three models would provide sufficient variability, we found that the development and application of stringent metrics, even ones limited to specific sectors, was not something the country teams were willing to take on (at least not voluntarily). Most of our interviewees remarked that while measuring progress is important, their country would be best served under an encouragement model as opposed to one that imposed accountable benchmarks in an MOA-like (binding) arrangement. We found some truth to these sentiments when we actually tried to group countries in one of three models—it was not an easy endeavor. We had difficulty finding examples where withdrawing or threatening to withdraw SJS assistance pressured a MENA country to meet benchmarks, nor did we find examples of MENA countries adopting a reform-oriented MOA with the United States. The closest example we found involved the Bahrain Independent Commission of Inquiry, which investigated the Bahraini government's response to protests in 2011 and provided recommendations for the government to reform the security and justice sectors. Although the commission was established by the King of Bahrain, it came about at least in part due to pressure from the United States, United Kingdom, and others in the international community.

In the MENA region in particular, some countries are in the process of transition, others show signs of possible transition, while still others show only the most modest signs of change. Ultimately, U.S. leverage—to the extent it exists—is extremely difficult to measure and continually shifts with changing political dynamics. In the end we determined that any new model should allow for flexibility in U.S. government planning to advance U.S. objectives in this region.

We opted to consolidate our three models into a single, hybrid model. Our consolidated model is centered on an enhanced planning approach that would draw on the most practical aspects of all three models, while maintaining sufficient flexibility for tailoring the approach to specific country nuances and needs. The model emphasizes the importance of benchmarks, but also that they must be developed through a *partner-owned* encouragement approach.

The new hybrid partnership model reflects what the team learned from its interviews, particularly from meetings with country teams and program/resource managers. We focus on planning aspects because we found some planning disconnects within embassy country teams, particularly in those countries where U.S. assistance is significant, and where similar types of programs are executed by different agencies. For example, we found some lack of coordination among agencies executing similar activities in the area of border security, where many U.S. government agencies run their own separate programs. Moreover, according to officials we spoke with, counterterrorism training programs run by the State and Defense departments do not always support the relevant organizations (in most cases, the Ministries of Interior) in the most appropriate ways. For example, in one country we found that the United States was providing the Ministry of Interior with equipment based more on U.S. supply than on partner nation requirements. In another country, ample Defense Department resources and a dearth of civilian agency resources meant that the partner country's counterterrorism efforts were overly focused on its military instead of the Ministries of Interior and Justice.

Complicated legislative restrictions and one-size-fits-all policies make it challenging to tailor programs to the specific needs of partner countries. We also found that performance and effectiveness assessments are not regularly occurring. While we heard the message from the field that stringent benchmarks linked to the release of specific SJS assistance packages are not politically feasible, most interviewees supported the idea that the United States could play a supporting role to partner country–established objectives and associated benchmarks. Table 3.2 outlines the defining principles for the proposed new hybrid model.

The Enhanced Partnership Planning (EPP) Model incorporates all of the characteristics of the SJS partnership concept described in Chapter One, and puts those characteristics into an actionable framework based on the fundamentals of strategic planning described here.

Table 3.2 organizes our principles in three categories: planning, assessing, and resourcing. We key on the term *partnership* to demonstrate how both the United States and the partner country have roles to play in all three categories. And in a true partnership, both parties have common objectives and shared responsibility and interests in the outcomes. Within planning, for example, the process should be iterative and focused. The United States should have a coordinated approach to planning in specific areas of interest to both sides before approaching the partner about the specific activities (thus the importance of vertical and horizontal integration).

In terms of assessing, it is the same general idea—specifically, that the United States should work tirelessly to bring partner country officials into the process by demonstrating the value of the assessing process, how assessments should inform decisionmaking, etc., so that the partner decides to take ownership of the process. There are also incentives for the partner. One is that additional U.S. resources often follow successful initiatives, and the assessment process can illuminate those initiatives. Another is that assessments can help to direct partner country resources—not only money, but manpower and time, as well.

For resourcing, decisions regarding resource allocation should be linked to and even driven by the assessment results. And the partner country should understand that this is not necessarily a "free good"—that, where appropriate, they are expected to identify ways to share burdens, particularly in the sustainment phases. Resource managers should be fully brought into the planning and assessing processes so

Table 3.2
Principles of an Enhanced Partnership Planning Model

	Model Key Principles
Planning	Horizontal (within embassy) and vertical (embassy to Washington, D.C.) integration
	Regular and iterative dialogue within U.S. government and with partner country officials
	Planning process informed by, but not necessarily constrained by, resource availability
Assessing	Decisions made on basis of well-informed and objective analysis; all parties have confidence in the process
	"SMART" objectives linked to specific metrics
	Benchmarks/milestones that are realistic and determined primarily by the partner country; partner country will not accelerate reforms based on an imposed timeline
	Opportunity to experiment and test theories
	Assessment results will trigger some kind of action (i.e., accountability)
Resourcing	Assessment results linked to resourcing decisions
	Resource managers are included in, and buy into, the existing planning and assessment processes
	Partner country may be responsible for some or all costs of start-up or sustainment activities

that they understand where they might continue, cut, alter, or even expand an existing activity to increase impact.

Implementing a New Approach: Opportunities

As Chapter One explains, the QDDR and the SSA PPD open up new opportunities for dialogue on a global scale on SSA and more effective and accountable diplomacy. Ongoing transitions in partner countries, particularly in the MENA region, create new conditions on the ground and new security realities, some of which are game-changers, enabling and, in some cases, even demanding a new U.S. government approach.

This sentiment links to the first key opportunity we see in the MENA region—the idea of changing the mantra from *security sector assistance* to *security and justice sector partnerships*, as we will discuss.

This subtle change, we think, better communicates U.S. expectations for the relationship. In other words, the relationship is one of give and take on both sides. The United States could communicate its expectations from the assistance it provides, as well as ensure that it is meeting its responsibilities to the partner to assist, where needed, in the most effective ways. It really should not matter if the country is a grant-receiver or a cash customer for U.S. training and equipment: The relationship is larger than this one variable. Finally, based on several interviews, we saw important opportunities—often underexploited—for coordination among other donors and actors in the region, some of whom were following innovative and well-coordinated practices. For example, we found the United Kingdom to be active in several MENA countries, often using low-cost, high-impact approaches to engagement. In one country, they had embedded advisers in several partner government ministries and although the United States and others were exchanging information, there appeared to be minimal collaboration.

A second opportunity is to capitalize on the growing demand for U.S. (and allied) support for effective and professional security and justice sectors. We do not see this as a case of applying U.S. standards in a cookie-cutter fashion, but rather, coming to agreement with the partner on best practices and standards that make sense for them, and assisting partners with instituting new programs and initiatives that enable a higher level of professionalization.

A third opportunity might be to experiment a bit with benchmarking in "noncritical" partner countries as test cases. These would include countries whose government leadership is generally receptive to, and socialized in, the idea of measuring and communicating its progress, and sees real value in doing so. A starting point would be to identify a few areas where the partner country really wants to make progress, such as SJS professionalization. The idea would be to limit the assessment to a few priority areas, develop SMART objectives and associated performance and effectiveness metrics, assign an objective team to monitor and evaluate progress, and develop a plan and a schedule to assess and communicate progress.

Implementing a New Approach: Challenges

Naturally, challenges exist to implementing any new approach. Some of these challenges are political in nature; others are more process-oriented. While many of these challenges can be overcome, it is important to assess each in terms of the pros and cons of continuing a status quo, "business as usual" approach to SJSA.

First, it was made clear during our discussions in the field that ongoing U.S. security interests often constrain U.S government aspirations to push new reform-oriented initiatives. For example, deterring Iran, furthering Israeli-Palestinian peace accords, maintaining operational access to bases and key waterways (e.g., Suez Canal), improving coalition operations and interoperability with U.S. forces, and supporting the U.S. industrial base through foreign military sales can be perceived as taking priority over introducing new reform initiatives.

Second, there is a strong temptation to continue with "business as usual," particularly in countries where U.S. political leverage is perceived to be weak, and in countries that are unaccustomed to receiving U.S. requests that are fundamentally different from the status quo. In practice, we found that country teams in the MENA region are generally reluctant to introduce new initiatives aimed at furthering reforms in the security and justice sectors if the demand for change is not made clear by the partner country governments. Moreover, we found strong resistance to any new approach that would include an assessment process linked to specific consequences. As mentioned previously in our discussions of the three models, most interviewees favored the least ambitious, less intrusive encouragement model—even in countries where U.S. assistance levels are high. There was an overall perception that a new partnership model would be imposed on the partner, despite reassurances as to the importance of developing jointly formulated benchmarks.

Third, the fundamental basis of the U.S. SJS relationship varies widely across countries in the MENA region. In the context of the Arab uprisings, interviewees raised questions about the amount of leverage the United States really has in this region, particularly with the cash customers in the Gulf, but even with the neediest, grant-receiving partner countries. And in countries where the situation has changed, is the United States obliged to respond? At a strategic level, many also raised concerns that the United States does not always know where the red lines lie (i.e., what issues are flexible? Negotiable?), which makes changing any agreed-to approach unattractive and politically dangerous.

Fourth, we found a lack of clear incentives to integrate U.S. government SJS/economic efforts with those of allies/other donors. To be sure, the sharing of information does take place on an ad hoc basis, but mainly in the context of improving transparency rather than outright coordination or integration. For example, the United States and the United Kingdom are aware of each other's initiatives in Bahrain, specifically those aimed at helping the government of Bahrain to implement the recommendations of the Bahrain Independent Commission of Inquiry report. But actually doing projects together with shared resources is not commonplace. Drawing on lessons from Northern Ireland, the United Kingdom has been focusing on justice sector, human rights, and forensics training (i.e., moving from confessions to evidence-based approach). The U.S. approach is broader, and some embassy teams have told us there are too many "pet projects" that are uncoordinated in the region. The United States often lacks the ability—or sometimes just the will—to embed advisers, compared to the United Kingdom and other allies, in partner country governments. This was ascribed to complications inherent in the legislative authorities for various programs and policies from Washington, D.C. One exception we found is in Bahrain, where the United States has embedded an adviser in the Ministry of the Interior to support police training. Thus, an area of possible overlap with the United Kingdom is in coordinating embedded advisers to facilitate forensic training of the police force. In other cases (in the Gulf in particular), we found that collaboration opportunities are limited because of competition between the United States and the United Kingdom in foreign military sales. The same story holds for other allies (such as France) in this region, particularly in the United Arab Emirates, Saudi Arabia, and Bahrain.

Fifth, managing congressional interests and expectations is a real challenge to some but not all countries in the MENA region. Egypt and Bahrain are very strong on the congressional radar. There have been persistent calls from prominent figures (such as John McCain and Patrick Leahy) to undertake a top-to-bottom review of U.S. assistance to Egypt to ensure that it is in line with U.S. strategic objectives and Egypt's actual security needs. This kind of scrutiny is likely to increase in the wake of the July 2013 events in Egypt—widely perceived to constitute a military coup—and the country's new timetable for democratic transition. It would be preferable for some of these questions to enter into the U.S.-Egypt security cooperation dialogue without Congress having to force the issue.

Implementing a New Approach: Best Practices

As mentioned in Chapter One, the QDDR identifies several best practices that should characterize U.S. development aid policy going forward. First among them is an emphasis on heightened transparency, monitoring, and evaluation of all U.S. assistance. Our interviews have shown that some U.S. government organizations, for example the Bureau of International Narcotics and Law Enforcement Affairs, USAID, and MCC have found initial successes with increasing monitoring and evaluation, as well as developing and applying benchmarks, but only when the partner country truly takes ownership of the process. These organizations have found that reform is not amenable to a transactional approach, which is consistent with the academic literature on democratic conditionality and foreign aid.[2] Also, some organizations, such as the MCC, have had more positive responses to the introduction of benchmarking for reforms in the area of technical assistance. After several years of funding reform-oriented projects through its lower tier ("threshold") funding channel, MCC determined that such efforts were effective only where they focused on technical and regulatory reforms rather than democracy.

---

[2] Organization for Economic Cooperation and Development, "The Paris Declaration on Aid Effectiveness and the Accra Agenda for Action," 2005/2008. For a useful summary of the debates over conditionality, see Nicolas van de Walle, *Overcoming Stagnation in Aid-Dependent Countries: Politics, Policies, and Incentives for Poor Countries*, Washington, D.C.: Center for Global Development, 2005.

As already indicated, a second best practice is to shift away from the language of donor and recipient. The emphasis here lies instead on the idea of entering into development *partnerships*, a concept that implies mutual responsibilities and obligations.

More specifically, the QDDR articulates the need to develop new models of development partnership characterized in the following terms:

- **country ownership,** with partner countries taking the lead in developing and implementing evidence-based strategies, as appropriate. In those countries where governments are strongly committed to development and democracy, country ownership means working much more closely with and through those governments; in all countries it means working closely and consulting with organizations and the people most directly affected by programs and activities.
- **mutual accountability,** creating mechanisms for meaningful commitments for action and resource allocation by both partner governments and donors.[3]

In practice, it has been difficult to integrate country ownership and accountability criteria into U.S. foreign assistance more broadly—a domain that traditionally has been heavily guided by political earmarks and strategic considerations.

Third, we found in our discussions with these organizations that human capacity development is the foundation for enabling long-term reform. Our interviews revealed repeatedly that security assistance programs focused on building human capacity are crucial for effecting sustainable reforms in the security sector and civil-military relations more broadly. Another recent study on defense cooperation with the region echoes this theme, urging the United States to "apportion less money to equipment purchases and more money to exercises, exchanges, and training—particularly IMET—that will help inculcate values of trans-

[3] U.S. Department of State and USAID, p. 110.

parency, accountability, and civilian control of the military."[4] Cases where the partner desires only the equipment and is less interested in the training are a little more tricky. Discussions with partner officials might emphasize the value of the training in enhancing the overall partnership with the United States.

Beyond advancing good governance, this emphasis on human capacity also helps to develop greater social capital in the security and justice sectors. Enhanced trust and reciprocity between various security actors and agencies in partner nations—as well as between the United States and its partners—may foster greater resilience in the face of crises and other security challenges, perhaps making it less likely that kinetic capabilities will need to be deployed.

Fourth, deliberate strategic planning exercises can help translate monitoring and evaluation efforts into programming changes. For example, one ambassador described his concern that the United States had led itself into a strategic dead end with its partner government. In response, the country team brought out an interagency team to rethink what the United States should try to achieve with the security forces of this country. The result of this planning exercise was a report back to Washington, D.C., describing a more effective engagement strategy that led to important programmatic changes. However, involving the partner country more directly in the process will not necessarily allow for an easy escape from this strategic dead end situation. In some cases, partners prefer to be in a strategic dead end relationship with the United States, as a way to ensure the United States will support them, regardless.

Core Themes from Our Interviews

This chapter began with a discussion of characteristics relating to several possible partnership models for the MENA region. By drawing on the most useful aspects of our three strawman models, we devel-

---

4 Casey and Kolbe, 2013, p. 19.

oped the framework for an Enhanced Partnership Planning Model to improve the impact of U.S. assistance in the following areas:

- **objectives**: More explicitly balancing objectives, including reform, and linking them to SJS activities; avoiding conditionality that would threaten the overall partnership
- **processes and stakeholder involvement:** Improving internal U.S. government coordination, including the incorporation of partner country planning, as well as ensuring partner country ownership of planning and project design
- **resources**: Maximizing investments (money, time, level of effort) in human capital programs, the foundation of persistent engagement
- **outcomes**: Integrating more rigorous monitoring and evaluation into the partnership, using a variety of assessment approaches (functional, technical, regional, country-specific) and linking SMART objectives to specific changes in SJS programs and activities.

The QDDR and the SSA PPD provide an opportunity to test the waters and to consider some new concepts as well as alternative options. The SJSP concept provides a more holistic way of thinking about efforts to harness security capacity-building to broader U.S. foreign policy goals while simultaneously reflecting some of the core principles and values contained in the QDDR and PPD.

In this chapter we have presented the broad findings of our research through an elaboration of the various SJSP models that informed our initial thinking on the report's key research questions. Based on consultation with a wide range of stakeholders, we then developed a single integrated model based on an analysis of challenges, opportunities, and best practices surrounding contemporary SSA. In Chapter Four, we will translate our findings and model development efforts into a set of concrete recommendations for future SJSP efforts in MENA in the aftermath of the Arab uprisings. We will also suggest that many of these same recommendations can form the basis for a new approach to SJSPs globally.

CHAPTER FOUR

Recommendations for Implementing the SJSP Approach

Our analysis has indicated that current practices in the realm of U.S. SSA can be improved going forward—particularly in light of new political realities in key regions such as MENA and in light of new policy guidance governing SSA. In the aftermath of the Arab uprisings, the United States has committed itself anew to fostering sustainable democratic reforms in the region amid ongoing political volatility and new security challenges. Current approaches to MENA security assistance are not optimized for U.S. and partner nation security interests, nor are they optimized for broader U.S. reform goals. New SSA guidance from the White House echoes principles first articulated by the State Department's QDDR in calling for an approach to SSA that is founded on sound strategic planning, integrated and consistent with interagency operations, and accountable in terms of incorporating clear performance indicators, assessing impact, and articulating consequences for nonperformance.

In the previous chapter, we outlined the broad contours of a new approach to what we termed security and justice sector partnerships. This was informed by our analysis of what is and is not working in current approaches; data collected; and interviews with a wide range of stakeholders, including U.S. government personnel, partner nation officials, nongovernmental organizations, and U.S. allies. The SJSP concept is founded on three interrelated principles: *planning*, *assessing*, and *resourcing*. In this final chapter, we will move from principles to action by laying out the key operational parameters of an EPP Model based on our insights, as well as to detail a number of actionable recommendations that follow from our SJSP principles.

SJSP is not a revolutionary concept. Rather, it is a way of emphasizing existing best practices through more rigorous and integrated planning, assessments, and resource management. As discussed in Chapter One, the five main components of SJSP are (1) more clearly and explicitly linking military and nonmilitary forms of security assistance; (2) emphasizing human capital development; (3) linking security sector reforms and broader governance reforms; (4) partner nation ownership of program objectives and evaluation criteria; and (5) practical benchmarks for measuring progress linked to SMART objectives.

The Enhanced Partnership Planning Model

The fundamental question underlying our investigation of new partnership models is the following: "How can the United States simultaneously deliver SJSA while also advancing reform objectives?" This question was particularly important in the context of the Arab uprisings. Our EPP Model puts the SJSP concept into action by focusing on improving collaborative planning, instead of trying to influence partner nations to do what the United States wants. Our interviews made it clear that partner nations neither accept nor reject U.S. objectives unquestioningly, but all value their relationships with the United States. Although these countries conduct planning exercises to various degrees, they are all consciously pursuing objectives. The EPP Model can support all five SJSP components, helping the United States and its partner nations pursue their objectives in a way that is more transparent and collaborative than is often the case now.

As discussed in Chapter Three, the EPP Model framework rests on three principles: planning, assessing, and resourcing. *Planning* refers to how stakeholders link objectives to activities and resources. Stakeholders include the members of the country team and those they connect to in Washington, D.C., and in the partner nation. Linking objectives to resources means identifying what the stakeholders are trying to achieve and explicitly describing how requested resources will help reach that goal.

In the context of our EPP Model, *assessing* refers both to an analysis of partner nation security and justice sector needs at the beginning of a planning cycle and to the evaluation of progress toward objectives at the end of a planning cycle. The needs assessment takes place prior to the start of a set of activities being implemented; evaluation takes place after activities have occurred and help inform the next cycle of planning.

Finally, *resourcing* refers to activities, personnel, and funding required to make progress toward objectives. While most of our discussion of resources focuses on U.S. SJSA, the partner nation also plays an important role in providing resources. As discussed in Chapter Two, many partner countries, including almost all MENA partners, purchase U.S. equipment and services through FMS, while all—regardless of national wealth—must invest some of their own people and funding to achieve their SJS objectives.

In effect, an EPP Model can be a vehicle by which the United States and the partner nation can clarify their objectives, assess what's required to advance toward those objectives, monitor and evaluate progress, and prioritize resource allocation. It may be a valuable way for the United States and its partners to improve both their internal coordination and their bilateral engagement. It can also facilitate regional cooperation.

The PPD on SSA identifies the State Department as the lead agency for SSA, responsible for the integration of interagency efforts, including interagency planning.[1] The State Department has developed an approach for implementing the SSA PPD that reinforces many of the components of our proposed EPP Model. This emerging approach improves upon past efforts at planning. For example, many interviewees argued that past planning documents, like the Mission Strategic and Resource Plans (MSRPs), were paperwork exercises that made little difference to decisionmaking. Country teams sometimes felt they had made good-faith efforts to base resource requests on strategic plan-

1 The White House, 2013.

ning and host nation engagement, only to receive allocations that bore little resemblance to their original requests. Should this happen under an EPP Model, which would also include greater partner nation participation, the diplomatic fallout of dashed expectations could be problematic. The State Department's new approach creates stronger links between regional, functional, and country-specific strategies on the one hand and resource requests on the other. Moreover, these strategic planning documents will be more closely tied to interagency decision-making processes, including through the Security Sector Assistance Interagency Policy Committee, led by the National Security Staff. In order to ensure that this new approach does not fall prey to some of the challenges surrounding the previous MSRP approach, it will be important for the interagency policy committee process that allocates sector-specific resources to track with the EPP as it evolves. Moreover, expectation management will have to be an integral component of such collaborative planning, with plans that can accommodate both successful and failed efforts to increase resources.

Our EPP Model is especially relevant to the integrated country strategies (ICSs), which the QDDR directed to be overarching strategies that "encapsulate U.S. government policy priorities, objectives, and the means . . . to achieve them."[2] The ICSs, which are also central to the SSA PPD, could serve as the primary vehicle by which the EPP Model could be implemented and documented, because it could serve as the centerpiece of collaborative planning. In effect, the ICS could be the connecting point for planning that occurs within the country team, between the country team and Washington, D.C., and between the country team and the partner nation. It could also document partner nation needs assessments, linkages between objectives and measures of progress, and linkages between assessments and resourcing decisions. The National Security Staff may have to lead an iterative process that indicates expected resource levels at the outset, with country teams then devising resource-informed (though not resource-driven) plans.

---

[2] U.S. State Department and USAID, 2012, p. 191.

From Principles to Action: Recommendations for SJSP Implementation

The EPP parameters we have described provide SSA program planners with broad guidelines that will help lay the groundwork for incorporating SJSPs into ICSs that are consonant with new SSA policy guidance. We now focus on concrete proposed actions that follow from our research and the EPP principles we have outlined. These compose a series of recommendations (see Table 4.1) for specific SSA activities and programmatic elements that embody the SJSP approach.

From Principles to Action: Planning

Although it can be confusing to include planning as a component of a planning model, we consciously emphasize planning as a core component of our EPP Model.[3] In this context, we are focusing on planning as the process by which stakeholders link objectives to activities and resources. It is a method for stakeholders to make these linkages by integrating their efforts and participating in a structured, iterative dialogue. Our research found that SSA planning was often conducted in a relatively ad hoc manner. Documents like the MSRP were weakened by a lack of effective processes to support them and thus were often perceived as paperwork exercises centered on existing resources, rather than planning exercises centered on strategy. The SSA PPD and its supporting documents provide an opportunity for country teams and other stakeholders to plug into more effective processes that will improve horizontal and vertical integration, so long as planning efforts remain tethered to broad resource parameters and can adapt to changes in resource allocations.

Needless to say, our interviews did not reveal a shortage of meetings. Rather, most concerns centered on the challenges of integrating

---

[3] The State Department does this as well, describing the SSA planning process as having four components: planning, budgeting, managing, and measuring. U.S. Department of State, *Plan to Implement a Security Sector Assistance Planning Process, 2013–2015,* September 18, 2013 [draft not publically available].

Table 4.1
Putting EPP Principles into Action

Phase	Model Key Principles	Proposed Actions
Planning	Horizontal (within embassy) and vertical (embassy to Washington, D.C.) integration	Set up a formalized structure to discuss SJS in specific sectors; consider quarterly meetings with senior officials, and monthly meetings with action officers
	Regular and iterative dialogue within U.S. government and with partner country officials	Explicitly establish ICSs as the focus of regular interagency and U.S. government–partner nation discussions about joint objectives and SJSP activities
	Planning process informed by, but not entirely constrained by, resource availability	Identify likely resource constraints as early as possible and mitigate negative effects by leveraging the efforts of other stakeholders
Assessing	Decisions made on basis of well-informed and objective analysis; all parties have confidence in process	Together with the partner country, identify key sectors and specific areas to assess progress
	Well-written objectives linked to specific metrics	Develop SMART objectives and metrics to assess progress; share with partner in a workshop to validate
	Benchmarks/milestones that are realistic and determined primarily by the partner country; partner country will not accelerate reforms based on an imposed timeline	In a workshop with the partner country, identify milestones (on a timeline)
	Opportunity to experiment and test theories	Together with partner, select a pilot project on a topic of mutual interest in SJS. For example, address deficiency in institutional capacity-building efforts
	Assessment results will trigger some kind of action (i.e., accountability)	Consider formalizing the approach in an MOA or a more flexible MOU to share with the partner; use the new ICSs to capture data and track progress
Resourcing	Assessment results linked to resourcing decisions	Ensure assessment results reach resource managers (with specific recommendations) in time to inform their decisions

Table 4.1—Continued

Phase	Model Key Principles	Proposed Actions
Resourcing	Resource managers are included in, and buy into, the existing planning and assessment processes; expectation management and resource planning that can adapt to either reductions or increases	Ensure resource managers take part in planning and assessing meetings with the partner
	Partner country may be responsible for some or all costs of start-up or sustainment activities	Communicate this in an MOU or other more formal communique

and prioritizing the overwhelming number of activities and ideas circulating at an embassy and in Washington, D.C. Adding in activities and ideas from the partner nation, other nations, and nongovernmental organizations multiplies the challenges facing U.S. planners, particularly those at the country team. Many who have spent time at a U.S. embassy understand why it might be frustrating to hear complaints that the country team is too reactive. While no planning model will eliminate the complexities of simultaneously managing programs and reacting to crises, the recent policy changes discussed in this report may provide an opportunity to strengthen the U.S. approach to SJSPs through improved planning structures and processes. Our model focuses on improving reviews of SJS programs—not by establishing more meetings, but by scheduling fewer and more systematic meetings organized by sector and directly tied into SSA planning and resourcing procedures that the State Department has just established.

Given the difficulties of integrating U.S. government planning, many country team officials are skeptical about the value of promoting partner nation planning. The State Department may wish to use the SSA PPD as an opportunity to change this dynamic. As ICSs become cornerstones of SJS planning, and as planning structures and procedures improve among U.S. SJS stakeholders, partner nation planning can more easily be incorporated. Eventually, ICS-based bilateral planning could grow into a foundational element of the U.S.–partner nation relationship. The ultimate objective would be to change the paradigm from pressuring a partner's reform to supporting the partner's own efforts to achieve planning benchmarks related to both reform and capability goals. While these are ambitious goals, the State Department is already taking some steps in this direction, based on QDDR and PPD-23 guidance. Improved coordination of the security and justice sector, improved links between objectives and resources, and improved assessments may facilitate more planning-focused engagement with partners. In other words, if the U.S. government improves its own planning, it will be more capable of planning with partners.

In light of these findings, we make the following recommendations with respect to planning for the EPP Model:

1. Establish a formalized structure for SJS discussions in specific sectors. Regular planning meetings under this structure would help integrate SJS stakeholders within each embassy, within Washington, D.C., and between the embassy and Washington. Such a structure could reduce ad hoc coordination and redundant meetings and could improve the focus of SJS efforts.
2. Building on the guidance from the SSA PPD, establish ICSs as the focus of regular discussions about joint objectives and SJSP activities. The ICSs are unlikely to be effective if—like many MSRPs—they are perceived as a paperwork exercise. The ICSs should be far more valuable if each country team explicitly uses them as a road map for both internal U.S. government and bilateral planning. The ICSs would not replace other agency plans, but rather help interagency planning, i.e., promote a dialogue that is far more important than any single document.[4]
3. As the SSA PPD improves linkages among objectives, activities, and resources, identify likely resource constraints as early as possible and mitigate negative effects. Mitigation can be accomplished, for example, by working with other stakeholders to leverage each other's efforts. These stakeholders include other

[4] Many USAID Country Development Cooperation Strategies are already annexes to ICSs, while the Department of Defense is using ICSs to guide development of Country Cooperation Plans.

U.S. government agencies, nongovernmental organizations, other donor nations, or the partner nation itself.

From Principles to Action: Assessing

Our focus on assessment as a core component of our EPP Model reflects both the QDDR's emphasis on greater accountability in U.S. foreign assistance as well as the more-detailed, sector-specific guidance found in the PPD on SSA. The latter stipulates a requirement for:

> Measurable security sector assistance objectives, appropriate data collection of the impacts and results of security sector assistance programs, and improved efforts to inform decision-making processes with data on what works and what does not work through impact evaluations when permissible.[5]

In the context of MENA and the post-Arab uprisings environment—with the United States placing greater emphasis on the importance of long-term reforms—integrating elements of assessment into SJSP program design can also serve as the basis for starting a dialogue with partner nations about the relationship between security cooperation, security sector reform goals, and broader reforms in other sectors. There are a variety of specific approaches that can be used to build assessment into SJSP, ranging from a minimalist model that seeks primarily to fulfill U.S. government criteria for greater coherence and accountability in SSA to mechanisms that link assistance to program performance and outcomes in various ways.

As our research has made clear, different approaches will be appropriate for different partner countries. Certain relationships in the region, where assessment has been mostly absent or constituted only a minimal aspect of SSA programs, will require a very gradual introduction of such concepts into operational paradigms. In other cases, where the relationship is different or where U.S. strategic interests demand it, consideration of more robust assessment mechanisms up front may

[5] The White House, 2013.

be advisable. In many cases, it will be possible to pursue a phased approach whereby strategic planning and the development of clear program objectives provide the basis for initial partner nation dialogues. Over time, and as the broader bilateral context permits, assessment elements involving greater specificity (and eventually, where appropriate, aspects of enforceability) can be introduced. Although assessments are labor- and resource-intensive, they are essential to effective program management. USAID, for example, recognizes this by requiring 3 percent of program funds be allocated for evaluations and recommending 5 to 10 percent of total program resources be allocated for monitoring and evaluation.[6] Agencies involved in dispensing SJS programs will need to continue developing their internal monitoring and evaluation capacity, independent from program implementation teams. This is an area in which USAID has invested heavily in recent years.

We make the following recommendations with respect to integrating assessment mechanisms into SJSP program design in ways that maximize partner nation ownership:

1. In dialogue with partner nation and based on common analysis of security sector priorities and needs, come to mutual agreement regarding key sectors and program areas that merit assessment to maximize outcomes and mutual benefit.
2. Once key SJSP sectors have been identified, apply SMART criteria to identify the possible metrics for assessing programs; share with partner nation in a workshop to validate and gain buy-in.
3. Together with partner, select a pilot project on a topic of mutual interest in the security and justice sectors. For example, address deficiency in institutional capacity building efforts.
4. Work with partner nation to identify specific benchmarks and timeline milestones ("check-in points") for the target project that both the United States and partner nation can use to assess performance and progress.

---

[6] USAID, ADS Chapter 203 "Assessing and Learning," November 2, 2012c, p. 24.

5. Where appropriate and where the broader bilateral relationship permits, consider formalizing the benchmarks and milestones in an MOU or, where practicable, in an MOA.
6. Integrate these steps and actions into ICSs to ensure that they reflect and remain deconflicted with broader U.S. strategic goals in the partner nation.

SJSP Principles into Action: Resourcing

For the most part, our research suggests that resources for the EPP Model are already in place through existing programs that are being executed in the MENA region. The key is to tie existing programs and activities to SJSP goals through SMART objectives. Moreover, when these activities are executed, they should be explicitly embedded within the broader context of the EPP Model. This approach would entail improving visibility and transparency among the program/resource managers to ensure that they are using their resources to build upon progress made in other activities and avoid redundancies.

As discussed in the description of the EPP Model, assessment results should be directly linked to resourcing decisions. Assessment results provide the wherewithal to make decisions regarding specific SJSP activities and whether they should be continued, modified, or cut, based on the impact they are actually having. To these ends, it is important to include resource managers on functional office staffs in the planning and assessment processes both within the U.S. team and with the partner country. Their inclusion in these processes should help ensure they are personally invested, their inputs are included, the results of the assessment are transparent to them, and, it is hoped, that resourcing decisions will reflect those results. More broadly, it is possible that the partner countries might provide some of their own national resources either to support the initiation of specific projects or perhaps to sustain them.

We make the following recommendations with respect to resourcing for the EPP Model:

1. Ensure assessment results reach resource managers and associated recommendation-makers in time to inform their decisions. Since some programs run on an annual cycle, some are multiyear, and some have midyear deadlines, these deadlines should be transparent to everyone.
2. Ensure that resource managers take part in planning and assessing meetings with the partner. This integration should be done in the earliest stages, including idea conception.
3. Communicate using an MOU or other more formal communique. While MOUs are nonbinding, they do provide a framework for moving forward. MOUs can help ensure that both U.S. and partner country officials are clear on the goals, objectives, milestones, assessment process, and resources available. This kind of transparency will help with managing expectations on both sides.

Looking Ahead: A New MENA in a Changing Global Context

In the future, it will also be important for the United States to recognize that its security cooperation efforts, not to mention foreign assistance efforts more broadly, proceed in the context of a global geopolitical framework undergoing important changes (and that the assistance programs contribute positively to such changes where possible). Primarily by virtue of their economic dynamism, there are now a wider set of players at the global table—including China, India, Brazil, and other so-called "emerging powers." Others in this category, while not quite economic giants, have indicated a willingness to assert a higher profile in international political and security affairs. Nations such as Turkey, Qatar, and Indonesia are relevant in this regard. To date, the U.S. policy response to this changing global environment has taken the form of a number of State Department-led strategic dialogues with countries such as India and China. The "rebalance to Asia" announced in 2011 can also be understood, at least in part, in this broader context of global power shifts in relation to both security risks and economic opportunities.

Much of the public debate about emerging powers has focused on the extent to which these countries pose a threat to the United States, or whether their rise is evidence of U.S. decline. Less attention has been paid to the question of whether and how the increased capacities and aspirations of certain nations might also represent a strategic opportunity for the United States. Some of these countries, such as South Korea, India, Brazil, and South Africa, can be thought of as "emerging donors" and have recently initiated modest aid disbursement programs. Indonesia has indicated a willingness to play a more active role in international security and peace-building efforts.

These developments have several implications for U.S. SJSP activities. First, they suggest that it may be possible to transcend the exclusively bilateral model that has characterized most U.S. security cooperation in the MENA region and elsewhere. For example, it may be possible for the United States to better achieve its strategic objectives in a given country or region by working in concert with one or many third-party nations whose interests and capabilities converge with both the United States and its SJS partners. Such an approach could have twin benefits, reducing some of the political sensitivities that often accompany partnerships with the United States while simultaneously reducing the direct U.S. burden in terms of money and human resources. There will also be times when the experience of third-party "emerging powers" will offer added value that the United States cannot bring to the table. For example, the Indonesian experiences with security sector reform, rebalancing civil-military relations, and control of corruption in the SJS potentially have direct and transferable relevance to the situation in Egypt today. Rather than viewing them exclusively as potential rivals, the United States should think about how the capacities of certain nations might complement U.S. efforts and represent significant opportunities for burden sharing.

Another area where there is potential for enhanced multilateralism and local ownership of SJSP activities relates to the human capacity dimensions of this work. Our research demonstrated that partnerships designed to enhance partner capacity within the human domain and to leverage the power of human relationships are viewed by multiple stakeholders as the heart of security cooperation. Military professionalization efforts, as advanced by IMET and other programs, emerged in our research as one of the most significant points of leverage for advancing U.S. strategic interests. Most of this work is conducted on a bilateral basis, whereby partner nations send officers to the United States for training and education. It may be possible to achieve a "force multiplier" effect for these activities by developing regional networks of civilian and military officials committed to good governance in SJS. Such networks would enable peer-to-peer learning, exchange of information about best practices, and the development of significant repositories of trust and social capital around responsible stewardship of security and justice affairs. Such an approach would also help refute the idea that norms of good governance are transferred exclusively from "donor" (the United States) to "recipient" (partner nation), and help reinforce the idea that there is a regional discussion about these issues with a life of its own. Awareness and participation in such networks can also help reform-minded security officials to feel more confident in pushing progress in their own countries, knowing that there are like-minded colleagues elsewhere in the region. The basic model for this approach comes from the world of U.S. democracy promotion, where efforts to create networks of key individuals committed to democratic reforms and accountable governance have been a standard part of the toolkit for more than a decade. More than anything, this regional networks approach has great potential to maximize, multilateralize, and regionalize the country ownership principle that is a hallmark of the SJSP concept.

Conclusion

There are always challenges, some of them daunting, associated with effecting significant changes to existing models for security cooperation in particular sectors—or with specific partner nations that have become used to certain ways of doing business. In the current climate, however, there are two significant impetuses to undertake a top-to-bottom shake-up of U.S. SSA in the MENA region. New guidance from the White House and State Department governing both U.S. foreign assistance at large, and security sector efforts more specifically, mandates important changes in how this kind of work is conceptualized, planned, and implemented in the future. At the same time, major regional developments suggest a clear strategic rationale for thinking and acting differently in the realm of SJSA.

Our research has revealed the limitations inherent in current SSA models and practices, and identified the contours of a new approach—captured in the SJSP concept—that can help to achieve the twin effects of integrating key principles behind new policy guidance even as it enhances the U.S. response to new regional, political, and security realities. We have provided a model that addresses opportunities, challenges, and best practices while preserving sufficient flexibility to accommodate the wide range of country nuances and bilateral equities found in the MENA region. We have explained how the core principles behind this model can be reflected in an enhanced approach to SJS program planning and laid out a set of specific recommendations for the planning, assessment, and resourcing of SJSP work.

While the scope of our work here has been relatively narrow, it has revealed a number of important areas that will likely require further attention in the near future. The new SSA PPD would benefit from a framework for implementing the guidance it promulgates in the MENA region. Such a framework could include the prioritization of SJSP activities that map to State Department objectives, or specifically those of the Bureau of Near Eastern Affairs, which would take stock of all SJSP activities that are planned and ongoing. It could also include the development of a monitoring and evaluation plan for SJSP in the MENA region, as well as the development of illustrative SJSP benchmarks, perhaps tailored to a few countries as test cases. A pilot effort could be launched to support the development of SJSP benchmarks in countries deemed amenable. Such an approach could serve as a solid proof of concept, as well as inform the development of the new ICSs.

This report in no way means to imply that better planning, better assessments, or even better resourcing can shape the MENA region in America's image. There is much the United States cannot and should not control in the realm of foreign affairs. There are also risks and opportunity costs to any changes in standard operating procedures. Nevertheless, U.S. policy guidance states—and experience shows—that there are opportunities to improve how the United States does business with its partners in the security and justice sectors. Our research consistently revealed the centrality of building and maintaining human relationships as a key factor in the success of these efforts, and, as the State Department embarks on a new QDDR exercise, this is an insight with broader implications that might merit additional attention.

Our primary goal in this report has been to provide a modest framework that can assist security and justice sector program planners to succeed in a rapidly changing operational context in which they are being asked to respond to intense regional volatility while simultaneously reconceptualizing and redesigning their work to incorporate significant changes in SSA policy guidance. Alongside what many will appropriately see as significant new challenges, we hope that the ideas and recommendations articulated throughout the report will help those who undertake this important work to appreciate the tremendous opportunities for SJSP that are also inherent in the Arab uprisings and broader global efforts to reform U.S. SSA.

Bibliography

Aftandilian, Gregory, *Egypt's New Regime and the Future of the U.S.-Egyptian Strategic Relationship*, Carlisle Barracks, Pa.: Strategic Studies Institute, U.S. Army War College Press, April 2013, p. 5.

Casey, George, and Jim Kolbe, *A New Deal: Reforming U.S. Defense Cooperation with Egypt, Libya, and Tunisia*, Washington, D.C.: Atlantic Council of the United States, 2013, p. 19.

Collier, Paul, "Is Aid Oil? An Analysis of Whether Africa Can Absorb More Aid", *World Development*, Vol. 34, No. 9, 2006, pp. 1482–1497.

Defense Security Cooperation Agency, *Foreign Military Sales, Foreign Military Construction Sales, and Other Security Cooperation Historical Facts*, September 30, 2012. As of March 18, 2014:
http://www.dsca.mil/sites/default/files/historical_facts_book_-_30_sep_2012.pdf

Dunning, Thad, "Conditioning the Effects of Aid: Cold War Politics, Donor Credibility, and Democracy in Africa," *International Organization*, Vol. 58, Spring 2004, pp. 409–423.

Fund For Peace, *Failed States Index*, web page, undated. As of July 2013:
http://ffp.statesindex.org/

Goldsmith, Arthur A., "Foreign Aid and Statehood in Africa," *International Organization*, Vol. 55, No. 1, 2001, pp. 123–148.

International Security Advisory Board, *Report on Security Capacity Building*, Washington, D.C.: U.S. Department of State, 2013, p. 1.

ISAB—*See* International Security Advisory Board.

Kirkpatrick, David, D., "For the United States, Arab Spring Raises Question of Values Versus Interests," *New York Times*, November 15, 2013.

Kleinfeld, Rachel, *Advancing the Rule of Law Abroad: Next Generation Reform*, Washington D.C.: Carnegie Endowment for International Peace, 2012.

Londoño, Ernesto, and Holly Yeager, "In Debate over Military Aid to Egypt, Contractual Issues Loom Large for U.S.," washingtonpost.com, July 25, 2013. As of March 18, 2014:
http://www.washingtonpost.com/world/national-security/in-debate-over-military-aid-to-egypt-contractual-issues-loom-large-for-us/2013/07/25/9d0834c0-f4a5-11e2-aa2e-4088616498b4_story.html

Marshall, Monty G., and Benjamin R. Cole, *Table 1: State Fragility Index and Matrix 2012*, Center for Systemic Peace, 2012. As of July 3, 2013:
http://www.systemicpeace.org/inscr/SFImatrix2012c.pdf

Mold, Andrew, *Policy Ownership and Aid Conditionality in the Light of the Financial Crisis: A Critical Review*, Development Centre Studies, OECD Publications: 2009.

Organization for Economic Cooperation and Development, "The Paris Declaration on Aid Effectiveness and the Accra Agenda for Action," 2005/2008. As of July 2013:
http://www.oecd.org/development/effectiveness/34428351.pdf

Sharp, Jeremy, *Jordan: Background and U.S. Relations*, Congressional Research Service, April 9, 2010.

Sherman, Jason, "'Arab Spring' Prompts DoD to Scrap $84M in Security Assistance to Partner Nations," *Newsstand*, Insidedefense.com, August 17, 2013.

Telhami, Shibley, *The World Through Arab Eyes: Arab Public Opinion and the Reshaping of the Middle East*, New York: Basic Books, 2013.

U.S. Agency for International Development, *Interagency Security Sector Assessment Framework: Guidance for the U.S. Government, Chemonics International, Inc.*, October 1, 2010.

———, ADS Chapter 200, "Introduction to Programming Policy," February 10, 2012a, pp. 22–32.

———, *3D Planning Guide, Diplomacy, Development, Defense*, July 31, 2012b.

———, ADS Chapter 203 "Assessing and Learning," November 2, 2012c, p. 24.

U.S. Department of State, "Manama Dialogue Opening Dinner," Remarks by Hillary Rodham Clinton, December 3, 2010. As of July 2013:
http://www.state.gov/secretary/20092013clinton/rm/2010/12/152354.htm

———, "Keynote Address at the National Democratic Institute's 2011 Democracy Awards Dinner," Remarks by Hillary Rodham Clinton, November 7, 2011. As of July 2013:
http://www.state.gov/secretary/rm/2011/11/176750.htm

———, *Plan to Implement a Security Sector Assistance Planning Process, 2013–2015*, September 18, 2013 [draft not publically available].

U.S. Department of State and U.S. Agency for International Development, *Leading Through Civilian Power, The First Quadrennial Diplomacy and Development Review*, 2010. As of July 2013:
http://www.state.gov/documents/organization/153108.pdf

U.S. Government Accountability Office, *Program Evaluation: Strategies to Facilitate Agencies' Use of Evaluation in Program Management and Policy Making*, Washington, D.C., GAO-13-570, June 2013.

USAID—*See* U.S. Agency for International Development.

van de Walle, Nicolas, *Overcoming Stagnation in Aid-Dependent Countries: Politics, Policies, and Incentives for Poor Countries*, Washington, D.C.: Center for Global Development, 2005.

Weber, Vin, and Gregory B. Craig, *Engagement Without Illusions: Building an Interest-Based Relationship with the New Egypt*, The Washington Institute for Near East Policy, 2012.

The White House, "Remarks by the President on the Middle East and North Africa," May 19, 2011. As of March 18, 2014:
http://www.whitehouse.gov/the-press-office/2011/05/19/remarks-president-middle-east-and-north-africa

———, "Presidential Policy Directive 23: Security Sector Assistance," April 5, 2013. As of July 2013:
http://www.whitehouse.gov/the-press-office/2013/04/05/fact-sheet-us-security-sector-assistance-policy

World Bank, *GDP*, web page, undated. As of March 18, 2014:
http://data.worldbank.org/indicator/NY.GDP.MKTP.CD

———, *Military Expenditures*, web page, undated. As of March 18, 2014:
http://data.worldbank.org/indicator/MS.MIL.XPND.GD.ZS

Interviews

Officials from the International Institute for Strategic Studies and several other nongovernmental organizations.

Officials from the government of Bahrain.

Officials from the United Kingdom Ministry of Defence, Foreign and Commonwealth Office, and embassy in Bahrain.

State Department officials in the Bureau of Political-Military Affairs, Bureau of Near Eastern Affairs, Bureau of International Narcotics and Law Enforcement, and the Office of Policy Planning.

U.S. embassy officials in Egypt, Bahrain, Saudi Arabia, the United Arab Emirates, Yemen, and Morocco.

U.S. government officials from the U.S. Agency for International Development, the Office of the Secretary of Defense, U.S. Navy Fifth Fleet, and Millennium Challenge Corporation.